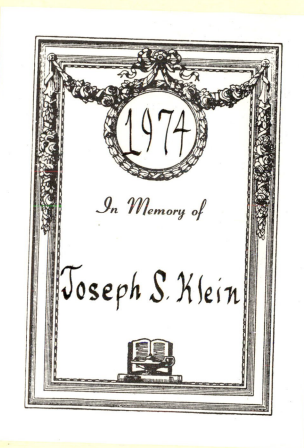

1974

In Memory of

Joseph S. Klein

PALESTRINA

Pope Marcellus Mass

An Authoritative Score

Backgrounds and Sources · History and Analysis

Views and Comments

NORTON CRITICAL SCORES

Giovanni Pierluigi da Palestrina

POPE MARCELLUS MASS

An Authoritative Score
Backgrounds and Sources · History and Analysis
Views and Comments

Edited by

LEWIS LOCKWOOD

PRINCETON UNIVERSITY

W·W· NORTON & COMPANY · INC · *New York*

Library of Congress Cataloging in Publication Data
Palestrina, Giovanni Pierluigi, 1525?–1594.
    Pope Marcellus Mass.
    (A Norton critical score)
    Bibliography: p.
    1. Masses—To 1800—Scores. 2. Palestrina, Gio-
vanni Pierluigi, 1525?1594. Missa Papae Marcelli.
I. Lockwood, Lewis, ed.   II. Title.   III. Series.
M2011.P25M38   1975   783.2'2'54   74–17020
ISBN 0–393–02185–8
ISBN 0–393–09242–9 (pbk.)

Contents

Introduction

More than any other composer of his age or of earlier times, Palestrina's reputation remained alive when the vast bulk of his contemporaries' music had largely passed into oblivion. Unlike the achievements of his contemporaries, therefore, his were largely obscured in later times not by neglect, but by attention—that is, the kind of attention that his name solicited for two centuries after his death, and in some circles long after that. In the periods before the rise of serious historical thought about music, Palestrina's posthumous reputation was based mainly on two firmly established beliefs. One was that he was the great master of the old art of vocal polyphony that later ages could formulate as a pedagogical technique called the "Palestrina style," successively refined in the course of time by theorists such as Fux, Bellermann, and Jeppesen. The other cast him in the role of the hero in history, the musician of genius whose timely intervention on behalf of high art saved polyphonic church music from a supposed ban threatened by the authorities of his time. Evidence for this is, of course, the mixture of legend and testimony that hovers over the work presented in this edition, and the durability of this story—itself a variant of the ancient myth of the power of music, the Orphean legend, in which the sixteenth century deeply believed—is visible in its dramatic retelling in the twentieth century in Pfitzner's allegorical opera *Palestrina*.

Thanks to the growth of historical scholarship in modern times, a more balanced and informed picture is now possible, and, if anything, the present danger is that Palestrina's importance in his own age may be undervalued. As scholars have transcribed and published the music of his predecessors and contemporaries, Palestrina's true relationship to the currents of his age has become much clearer, and it is now evident that in many sectors of his work—certainly in his Masses—he is not at all an isolated figure, but is profoundly dependent on the achievements of earlier composers. This is true in his Masses in a highly specific sense— of his 104 Masses, 31 are based on known compositions by earlier composers—but it is also true in a wider sense in other areas of his vast output. Although the *Pope Marcellus Mass,* the most famous of his Masses, is not based on a pre-existent composition, it requires elucidation in the light of its historical setting and the nature of Mass composition as an artistic problem in the sixteenth century. It also requires elucidation with regard to attributes of the musical system from which it springs —its tone system, notation, rhythmic and mensural organization, explicit accidentals and *musica ficta,* as well as means of composition—aspects that are largely unfamiliar to contemporary musicians steeped in the traditions of tonal music.

To clarify the historical setting and to enable the reader to perceive the exact nature of the historical problems surrounding this famous work, I have provided a section of source material that includes, in translation, a selection of the most important early documents bearing on the question of the origins of the Mass. The first segment contains documents from Palestrina's mature lifetime (between 1549 and 1575) while the second, with material from 1607 to 1828, contains important writings of later times on the same subject, mingling fact, hearsay, and tradition and showing the spread of the work's legendary reputation.

To clarify a number of problems of structure and interpretation from the historian's, analyst's, and performer's points of view, I have also provided a series of brief comments on relevant aspects of the work: its sources, performing forces, clefs, mensural organization and barring, accidentals, and musical structure. All of these are discussed under the heading "Notes on the Text and Structure of the *Pope Marcellus Mass,*" which is meant to complement the essay by Knud Jeppesen in the volume. In writing these "Notes" I have had in mind principally the performer and reader for whom these aspects of sixteenth-century music may be new or unfamiliar, adding references to more extended discussions of these topics.

While this volume was in proof, I learned of the death of Knud Jeppesen on June 14, 1974, at the age of eighty-two. With his passing, the world of musicology has lost one of its central modern figures, a scholar whose contributions to 16th-century studies, in particular, were of great scope and of fundamental significance. I regret that he did not live to see this small volume, which owes so much to his work both directly and indirectly, and which benefited from his valuable critical scrutiny of my translation of the article by him contained therein. This article ranks as the major essay thus far written on this Mass. The present second part of the article was originally published in German in 1929, and was reprinted in 1945 with the addition of the present first part. With the exception of one or two minor alterations and editorial footnotes (clearly marked as such, of course) that reflect discoveries or commentary since 1945, the version given here is a straightforward translation of the complete article as published in *Acta Musicologica*.

A word is needed regarding the title we are using for the Mass. The original title, *Missa Papae Marcelli,* could be literally translated as "Mass of Pope Marcellus." But most modern historians, with only a few exceptions, use the formulation given here, which is equivalent to the traditional German "Marcellus-Messe." I hope that purists will forgive my avoidance of the possessive in favor of the present title, which seems to me both brief and to the point.

I would like to acknowledge my indebtedness to the Civico Museo Bibliografico Musicale of Bologna and its librarian, Sergio Paganelli, for access to source material. I am grateful to David Hamilton for his original invitation to contribute this volume to the Norton Critical Scores series, and especially for his patience and his valuable editorial suggestions. I am also indebted to Claire Brook and the staff of W. W. Norton & Company for seeing the volume through its final stages.

Lewis Lockwood

BACKGROUNDS
AND SOURCES

In this section, all footnotes, unless otherwise identified, are by the editor.

Palestrina: A Biographical Note

Giovanni Pierluigi da Palestrina (born in Palestrina or Rome in 1525 or, at the latest, by February 1, 1526; died in Rome, February 2, 1594) was known throughout his lifetime by the surname "Prenestino" or "Palestrina" (the name of his family's native town in the Sabine hills near Rome) or by the familiar name "Gianetto." His musical training began in Rome where, in 1537, he was a choirboy at the basilica of Santa Maria Maggiore. His earliest teachers probably included the music masters at Santa Maria Maggiore from 1538 to 1540—Rubino Mallapert in 1538–39, a certain "Robert," and Firmin Le Bel in 1540—and it is significant that at least two of these (Mallapert and Le Bel) were French, and later served at San Luigi dei Francesi, the French church in Rome and an important musical center.

From 1551 until his death Palestrina's career, after a period of service as organist in his native town, centered entirely at Rome—the papal Rome of the Counter Reformation—and was steeped in the musical and liturgical traditions of three of the oldest and most celebrated of Roman churches, in all of which he held appointments: Santa Maria Maggiore, San Giovanni in Laterano, and San Pietro. But he was also a Roman in the urban sense, involved in matters concerning his fellow musicians of the city, and sufficiently practical-minded to manage a family and handle business matters rather adeptly.

In 1550 Cardinal Giovanni Maria del Monte, then bishop of Palestrina but also a notable figure in church politics, was elected Pope Julius III, and in September, 1551, he appointed Palestrina, then twenty-six, maestro of the Cappella Giulia, the musical chapel maintained by the chapter of the Basilica of San Pietro in Vaticano. In return, Palestrina's First Book of Masses (1554) was dedicated to the pope and contained a

Mass for him. In 1555 Julius installed him as a member of the pontifical choir (the "Cappella Sistina") despite his being married (a violation of its rules), without the usual entrance examination, and without the consent of its members. A few months later Julius died, succeeded by Cardinal Marcello Cervini, who took the name of Pope Marcellus II and for whom the *Pope Marcellus Mass* was named when it appeared in Palestrina's Second Book of Masses in 1567. Marcellus reigned for only three weeks before his death on May 1, 1555, in turn being succeeded by Pope Paul IV (1555–59), an intransigent reformer. His rigorous enforcement of reform measures resulted in, among other things, Palestrina's dismissal from the pontifical choir in September, 1555.

From 1555 to 1560 he was *maestro di cappella* at San Giovanni in Laterano, and from 1561 until about 1566 he held the same post at Santa Maria Maggiore. During the 1560s he also taught at the Roman seminary and was at various times in the private service of Cardinal Ippolito d'Este, taking charge of music in the summers at the Villa d'Este, the cardinal's sumptuous country estate outside Rome. In 1571 he returned to the Cappella Giulia as maestro, holding this post until his death. He thus remained in Rome throughout his mature life, rejecting offers of distinguished posts at the imperial court at Vienna (1567) and the ducal chapel at Mantua (1583). His great reputation was far from being purely posthumous, for in his later years he was held in awe by musicians as well as laymen. In 1575 he was described as being "now considered the very first musician in the world" (*hora stimato principalissimo musico tra quanti ne sono al mondo*), and in the early seventeenth century many theorists, especially Cerone (*El Melopeo y Maestro*, 1613), lauded him above all others. In 1592 an anthology of Vespers psalms by Italian composers was published in his honor with a glowing dedication by its editor, the prolific north Italian composer Gian Matteo Asola. Clearly his reputation was far from being confined to Rome.

His securely attributed works include 104 Masses (not 105 as sometimes stated), more than 250 motets, 68 Offertories, 45 hymns, 33 Magnificats, 4 or 5 sets of Lamentations, plus other pieces on sacred Latin texts; but also more than 140 madrigals. During his lifetime his principal publications included six volumes of Masses (1554–94), five books of motets, four volumes of madrigals, and, in his last years, a set of single volumes containing cycles of works for the liturgical year. This final group, a kind of *summa*, includes the Lamentations (1588), Hymns (1589), Magnificats (1591), Offertories (1593), and Litanies (1593). Beyond this, many works were left in manuscript at his death. The first truly comprehensive *catalogue raisonnée* of his works and their sources was made by Knud Jeppesen in his article *Palestrina* in *Die Musik in Geschichte und Gegenwart*, X (1962), cols. 663–83.

The list of patrons to whom his works were dedicated reveals a broad acquaintance with Italian courts and musical centers in northern Italy, especially Mantua, with which he had special ties through his long correspondence with Duke Guglielmo Gonzaga. That he had at least some publishing ties to Venice is suggested by certain publications and by the remarkable rapidity with which his works were issued during his lifetime by Venetian presses, often following immediately upon their appearance at Rome. Further evidence of the breadth of his knowledge of the music of his own time as well as that of earlier generations, going back to Josquin, is provided by the models chosen for his Masses based on preexistent polyphonic works. Of those identified so far (all but three), twenty-two are based on motets, five on madrigals, and one on a chanson. Their composers include prominent French, Flemish, and Spanish musicians of the period after Josquin who had been assimilated into papal and other Roman musical circles from 1513 onward—e.g., de Silva, L'Héritier, Penet, Morales; but also purely French figures not known to have been in Italy, such as Moulu and Maillard; and prominent composers active in northern Italy, such as Jaquet of Mantua and Cipriano de Rore. The tendency of traditional biographers to deal with Palestrina as an isolated figure is nowhere more misleading than in study of his Masses. And his relation to the world of his time was no doubt intensified by the status of Rome as a diplomatic center, swarming with foreign churchmen, ambassadors, and others who may be assumed to have had some role as patrons of music.

Palestrina's work has been issued in two major editions: (1) the *Werke,* published by Breitkopf & Härtel, Leipzig, in thirty-three volumes (1862–94), edited principally by F. X. Haberl, with earlier volumes edited by T. de Witt, F. Espagne, J. N. Rauch, F. Commer; (2) the *Opera Omnia,* (1938–) edited by R. Casimiri and, since his death, by Lino Bianchi, with individual volumes edited by L. Virgili and K. Jeppesen— it has so far reached thirty-two volumes.

Contemporary Documents
(1549-75)

This section provides, in translation, an annotated selection of the earliest documents that bear on the question of the origins of the *Pope Marcellus Mass*. Stemming from sources of very different kinds, they form a heterogeneous body of historical evidence that sheds more light on the background of the Mass than on the specific problem of the date of its origin. Nevertheless, they constitute the vast bulk of the known evidence from within the composer's lifetime that is relevant to this question, and as a basis for critical evaluation of the later source readings in this volume— especially those of the period 1607 to 1828, from Agazzari to Baini—they are essential. Close reading of these documents should enable the reader to judge for himself what is known and what is unknown about the circumstances in which the work was composed, and should help him to evaluate the conclusions drawn by later writers based on what they knew of such evidence from earlier times. My hope is that this material may stimulate further study and research on the problem, but even more, that it may provide a sample of the cumulative character of historical judgment and explanation. In that sense the importance of these documents goes beyond this work, this composer, and this period in the history of music.

To clarify these documents, they are preceded by a brief chronology of events that link Palestrina to papal actions concerning church music during this period.

Palestrina	*The Papacy and Sacred Music*
	1545: Council of Trent begun (concluded in 1563)
	1550: February—Election of Pope Julius III (Cardinal Giovanni del Monte, bishop of Palestrina)

Palestrina

1551: September 1—Palestrina named master of the chapel at the Cappella Giulia (San Pietro, Rome)

1554: Publication of First Book of Masses, dedicated to Pope Julius III.

1555: January 13—Palestrina admitted as singer to pontifical choir at Pope Julius's request, without entrance examination, without consultation of the members, and even though he was married.

1555: September—Palestrina dismissed from pontifical choir by Pope Paul IV with two other married singers.

1555: October 1—Appointed master of the chapel at San Giovanni in Laterano, Rome.

1561: Appointed master of the chapel at Santa Maria Maggiore, Rome.

The Papacy and Sacred Music

1555: April 9—Election of Pope Marcellus II (Cardinal Marcello Cervini), who reigned for twenty days (April 10 to April 30). (For evidence of his interest in sacred music, see Reading 3, p. 78.)

1555: May 23—Election of Pope Paul IV (Giovanni Pietro Caraffa)

1559: December 25—Election of Pope Pius IV (Giovanni Angelo Medici);

1560: Appointment of Cardinal Carlo Borromeo as papal secretary of state and archbishop of Milan (resident in Rome, 1560–65).

1561–62: Exchange of music between Rome and the court of Munich, involving Cardinals Borromeo and Vitelli in Rome and Duke Albrecht V of Bavaria, with Cardinal Truchsess von Waldburg as go-between. Music of Lassus sent to Rome; music of Palestrina and François Roussel sent to Munich.

Palestrina

The Papacy and Sacred Music

1562: Subject of sacred music taken up at Council of Trent (see Reading 4, p. 19); decree on suitability of church music released.

1563: Publication of First Book of Motets.

1563: Conclusion of Council of Trent.

1564: Appointment of Commission of Cardinals by Pope Pius IV to carry out decrees of Trent within Rome (members included Cardinals Borromeo and Vitelli).

1565: Commission of Cardinals (January–August, 1565) negotiates with singers of papal chapel on size of its membership, salaries, and regulations. Cardinal Borromeo (January–March, 1565) corresponds with his vicar in Milan, Niccolò Ormaneto, on problem of "intelligible sacred music," and orders a Mass to be composed by the master of the chapel at the Cathedral of Milan, Vincenzo Ruffo, which should be sent to Rome for comparison with other works (see Reading 5, p. 20).

1565: April 28—Entry in diary of papal chapel on testing of "certain Masses" for intelligibility at home of Cardinal Vitelli (see Reading 6, p. 21).

1565: October—Palestrina paid by papal chapel for "various musical compositions that he has had copied for the chapel and is to have copied."

1565: September—Cardinal Borromeo leaves Rome permanently for Milan.

Palestrina

1567: Publication of Second Book of
Masses (containing *Pope Marcellus
Mass*), dedicated to King Philip
II of Spain (see Reading 7, p.
22).

Contemporary Documents
(1549-75)
READING 1
BISHOP BERNARDINO CIRILLO

[Letter to Messer Ugolino Gualteruzzi] †
1549

Bishop Bernardino Cirillo, also known as Cirillo Franco (c. 1500–75), was a reputable figure in Italian ecclesiastical circles of the mid-sixteenth century. He was rector of the famous shrine of the Santa Casa of Loreto from about 1540 to about 1555; from 1556 to 1575, at Rome, he was a canon of Santa Maria Maggiore and *commendatore* of the Arcispedale di Santo Spirito. His letters reveal a gift for rhetorical expression along with ponderous erudition. The recipient of the present letter, Ugolino Gualteruzzi, was in the employ of Lodovico Beccadelli, bishop of Ravello, himself a literary man of importance, and a close friend of Cardinal Marcello Cervini, later Pope Marcellus II.

For many years my mind has been burdened with an idea that, for lack of ability to express it, has almost stopped the flow of my thoughts. Now I am determined to bear it no longer on my brain, and, as best I can, I propose to portray it for you in this letter with the aim and hope that you will read in it much more than I shall write to you, and that, thanks to your fine understanding, you will formulate my idea in your mind— for I cannot give a complete exposition of it, but can only sketch it out.

† From Aldo Manuzio, *Lettere Volgari di Diversi Nobilissimi Huomini . . . Libro Terzo*, Venice, 1564, pp. 114–18. Translated for this volume by the editor. Another version of the letter, differing in a few details, was published from a contemporary manuscript source in P. de Angelis, *Musica e Musicisti nell'Arcispedale di Santo Spirito in Saxia*, Rome, 1950, pp. 39–44.

Now the subject is this—that music among the ancients was the most splendid of all the fine arts. With it they created powerful effects that we nowadays cannot produce either with rhetoric or with oratory in moving the passions and affections of the soul. With the power of song it was easy for them to drive a wise mind from the use of reason and bring it to a state of madness and willfulness. By this means it is said that the Lacedaemonians were incited to take up arms against the Cretans; that Timotheus was roused against Alexander; that a young man of Taormina was induced to set fire to the house in which his beloved was concealed; that in the sacrifices of Bacchus people were roused to frenzy; and similar effects.[1] And the mode or species that incited this state of mind was called Phrygian.

To this species there was opposed another, called Lydian, with which men could be easily withdrawn from the condition of frenzy and madness into which they had been plunged by the first kind of music.

The third was called Dorian, which attracted and moved the affections of the soul to gravity and modesty, and with so much strength and force that it was not only difficult, but almost impossible for anyone hearing it to bend his spirit toward a vicious or ignoble action. They say that Agamemnon, on going to the Trojan Wars, left a Dorian musician with his wife Clytemnestra, whose task it was, by means of his music, to charm her away from infidelity; and Aegisthus could not corrupt her until he had the musician murdered.[2] This kind of music was always highly valued and esteemed.

Then we have the fourth species, called Mixolydian, by which anyone hearing it was immediately moved to tears, cries, and lamentation; this was used for sad and mournful occasions.

See, my Lord, what a splendid thing this is! By means of the power of song a slow and lazy man becomes lively and active; an angry man is

1. These anecdotes, illustrating the power of music, were well known to Renaissance writers. On the tale of the Lacedaemonians see the excerpt from Baldassare Castiglione's *Book of the Courtier* in Oliver Strunk, *Source Readings in Music History*, New York, 1950, p. 283. On Timotheus and Alexander see, among other writings, Strunk, *ibid.*, pp. 82, 282, 319; Erwin Panofsky, "Who Is Jan van Eyck's 'Timotheus?'" in *Journal of the Warburg and Courtauld Institutes*, XXI (1949), 80–90; and for many other references to Timotheus in English literature see John Hollander, *The Untuning of the Sky*, New York, 1970, pp. 412–20.

2. The tale of Clytemnestra and the musician is apparently derived by later writers from the *Odyssey*, 3, 267 f., and from commentaries on Homer. See W. H. Roscher, *Ausführliches Lexikon der Griechischen und Römischen Mythologie*, II, Leipzig, 1890–94, p. 1235.

calmed; a dissolute man becomes temperate; an afflicted man is con-
soled; a miserable man becomes happy; and thus music governs human
affections and has the power to alter them as need be. Now, where has
this led?

I see and hear the music of our time, which some say has been
brought to a degree of refinement and perfection that never was nor
could be known before.[3] And yet I neither see nor hear any of the afore-
said ancient modes, and testimony to this is given by the movements of
the soul that arise from it (perhaps you will say to me, "Shoemaker,
stick to your last"). This much is clear—that the music of today is not
the product of theory, but is merely an application of practice. *Kyrie
eleison* means "Lord, have mercy upon us." The ancient musician would
have expressed this affection of asking the Lord's pardon by using the
Mixolydian mode, which would have evoked a feeling of contrition in
the heart and soul. And if it had not moved the listener to tears, at
least it would have swayed each hardened mind to piety. Thus he would
have used similar modes in accordance with the words, and would have
made a contrast between Kyrie and Agnus Dei, between Gloria and
Credo, Sanctus and Pleni, psalm and motet. Nowadays they sing these
things in any way at all, mixing them in an indifferent and uncertain
manner. And then, you see what they invariably do. They say, "Oh, what
a fine Mass was sung in chapel!" And what is it, if you please? It is
L'homme armé, or *Hercules Dux Ferrariae* or *Philomena.*[4] What the
devil has the Mass to do with the armed man, or with Philomena, or with
the duke of Ferrara? What numbers, what intervals, what sounds, what

3. A contemporary claim that music was in a constant process of improvement
over its previous level of achievement was advanced only a few years after the writing
of this letter by Nicola Vicentino, *L'antica musica ridotta alla moderna prattica,*
Rome, 1555, p. 10.

4. The famous *L'homme armé* melody of the fifteenth century, the origins of
which are still obscure, served as the basis for a long series of Mass settings by well-
known composers, ranging from Dufay and Ockeghem to Palestrina (who wrote two
settings) and beyond; the last setting is by Carissimi. The version perhaps closest in
time of composition and publication to the writing of this letter is the second setting
by Cristóbal de Morales, published in 1544 while Morales was a member of the papal
chapel. *Hercules Dux Ferrariae* refers to the well-known Mass composed by Josquin
Desprez for Duke Ercole I d'Este of Ferrara (reigned 1471–1505), in which the basic
musical subject of the composition is derived from the name of its recipient by using
the solmization syllables corresponding to the vowels in the name *Hercules Dux Ferrariae (re–ut–re–ut–re–fa–mi–re).* Later "Hercules" Masses were written in honor of
the second duke of this name, Duke Ercole II d'Este of Ferrara, and Cirillo's reference is probably to one of these. *Philomena* refers to the Masses by Gombert, Claudin
de Sermisy, and others based upon the motet by Jean Richafort on the text *Philomena
praevia.*

motions of the spirit, of devotion, or piety can be gathered from them, and how can music agree with such subjects as the armed man or the duke of Ferrara? Now, my dear Lord, read what little I have said and draw your own conclusions, for what I say of the music of the church I say of all other music as well. When I reflect upon ancient music in comparison with music of today, I see nothing of value but the pavane and the galliard, at the sound of which those good ladies of San Rocco and of Piazza Lombarda begin their movements, and it almost seems that they are listening to the Dionysiac dithyramb.

I consider the painting and sculpture of Michelangelo Buonarroti to be a miracle of nature; but when he decided to depict the scene of *Posteriora mea videbis* on the ceiling of the Sistine Chapel to show his ability in painting—and also so many nude figures, which he made in order to show off his skill—he might have done much better to paint them in the loggia of some garden, where it would have been more appropriate.[5] The quartered cloak was suitable attire for Captain Todeschino of the lancers when he was jousting, but when worn by our friend it is abominable; and nevertheless the cloak by itself is admirable. "The shoes are excellent, but they do not fit Socrates."

I should like, in short, when a Mass is to be sung in church, the music to be framed to the fundamental meaning of the words, in certain intervals and numbers apt to move our affections to religion and piety,[6] and likewise in psalms, hymns, and other praises that are offered to the Lord. And in the pavane and galliard, if the numbers and cadences they have are not sufficient, then let others be added to them so that they may be made to dance up to the very walls of the houses. Each mode should be adapted to its subject, and when one has a lullaby to sing, or a plaintive song, one should do likewise. Thus the musicians of today should endeavor in their profession to do what the sculptors, painters, and architects of our time have done, who have recovered the art of the ancients; and the writers, who have reclaimed literature from the hell to which it was banished by corrupt ages; and as the sciences have been explained and given in their purity to our times.[7] Thus the musicians

5. On this criticism of Michelangelo's *Last Judgment*, see J. Shearman, *Mannerism*, London, 1967, pp. 167 f.

6. For one of the most authoritative statements of this view by a contemporary music theorist, see the excerpt from Gioseffo Zarlino's *Istituzioni armoniche*, 1558, Bk. IV, Chap. 32, as translated in Strunk, *op. cit.*, pp. 256 f.

7. Among a number of similar claims by writers on painting and literature of this time one can cite, as perhaps the best known, Giorgio Vasari's description of painting as having undergone a "second birth" after its apogee in classical antiquity and its

should seek to recover the styles and modes, and the power of the Phrygian, Lydian, Dorian, and Mixolydian compositions, with which they would be able to do what they wish. I do not say that they should try to recover the enharmonic, diatonic, and chromatic genera, for these were dismissed by the ancients themselves; [8] but that they should approximate as much as possible the four above-mentioned modes, and that they should lend beauty and individuality to sacred music. In our times they have put all their industry and effort into the writing of imitative passages, so that while one voice says "Sanctus," another says "Sabaoth," still another says "Gloria tua," with howling, bellowing, and stammering, so that they more nearly resemble cats in January than flowers in May.[9] I hope that you will bear with me.

Now to conclude, for it is time. Again, where has this led? You, my Lord, are in Rome (Who knows? Sometimes things are first thought, then they are uttered, and at last at times they are even done), where it is imagined that there are men gifted with all wisdom. See if you can find there some good, genial, and willing musician who is accustomed to reasoned discourse, and discuss this letter a bit with him. Impress upon him the idea of what the ancients achieved, and that today no such effects are known, for today everything follows a single mold, always in the same way. Thus let us see if certain corrupt practices could be banished from the church, and if some music could be introduced that would move men to religion, piety, and devotion. And if they should say that they are only guided by plainsong, I would not be concerned (be it said with sincerity and reverence) if they should depart from that kind of music, in which one recognizes less of that power but can add a great deal more if only one would apply himself to recovering the ancient art. I believe so strongly in the ingenuity of our men of today that it seems to me that they can penetrate wherever they will. And if anyone should say to me, "Your idea is not new, it has been said before by others and attempted by musicians," I would reply that I observe the world to be dedicated to that which it does, and not what it ought to do, and I believe that musicians follow the same path.

---

decline in the dark ages that followed. Exactly the same view is espoused by Zarlino in the *Istituzioni armoniche,* in which he refers to ancient music as "somma altezza," to medieval music as "infima basezza," and to his revered teacher, Adrian Willaert, as having restored music to its ancient perfection in modern times.

8. Only a few years later an attempt was made to realize precisely this aim, with the publication of Vicentino's *L'antica musica ridotta alla moderna prattica.*

9. The original text is "che alle volte rappresentano un Gennaro di gatti, & un Maggio di fiori per non dire altrimenti."

Now my thought has been uttered, after long suppression. And if it has been voiced at other times, let this serve as reminder of it. Let him value it who can; it will help and not hurt him, and may the reader and listener have less fatigue in reading it than I have had in writing it. Not only do I absolve the musicians from hearing it, but I absolve you, my Lord, from reading it. For it was never my intention to be a nuisance to anyone, even if I am, as it turns out, a great nuisance to everyone, in appearance, word, and deed. But that is beyond my intention, as was the gossip of Aesop's ass.

If this discourse seems to you reasonable, say a word on its behalf to Signor Beccadelli. He, who has labored so much over his *Cosmography* for the benefit of the public, may labor too on this matter, to see to it that the praises of the Lord are sung well and in a manner different from those of secular texts. For this is all that stirs me: let them make their motets, chansons, madrigals, and ballate in their own way, as long as our church bends its own efforts to move men to religion and piety. My Lord, I assure you as I honor you, that it is now twenty years that I have had this notion on my mind, and as a man outside that profession and ignorant of it, I have never had the courage to express it. At other times I have read all of Plato superficially; and for many years one passage of his has remained with me to this day. You will find it in the third book of the *Laws*.[10] . . . Now this is done. I could not suppress it. Look and see, my Lord, whether there is someone in that court who is capable of what has been said, and see if our church music could retreat within the limits of these procedures, or could at least shed its more demeaning aspects. Then the wonderful ingenuity of the men of our day would penetrate into areas into which it has not yet entered. I have heard a madrigal by Arcadelt in which the voices exclaim most passionately, "Chi mi tiene il mio ben, che me l'asconde?" in certain numbers and cadences that are so expressive that they make these words speak, even though they do not really speak.[11] And at times one hears similar fine

10. Omitted in this translation but quoted in its entirety in Cirillo Franco's letter is a lengthy passage from Plato's *Laws*, Book III, on the categories of music that are suitable to different expressive purposes. On Lodovico Beccadelli see the headnote to this section; also the extended article on him in *Dizionario Biografico degli Italiani*, VII, Rome, 1965, 406–13.

11. Professor Albert Seay, editor of the complete works of Arcadelt for the series *Corpus Mensurabilis Musicae*, published by the American Institute of Musicology, kindly identified this work for me as being Arcadelt's setting of "Ahime dov' è'l bel viso," from his First Book of Madrigals for Four Voices, first published in 1538 or 1539. The text as quoted by Cirillo is not quite accurate, but is very close to that of

passages, so that I would not doubt that the study of such passages would lead to still others and to greater ones.

Now my thoughts are spoken; and I am free of them. Since they are departed from my own mind, they may enter into yours, and you must bend every effort to move them still further. And just as I have invited Signor Beccadelli, so I would also invite your master to consider them, but I know that both of them have more pressing concerns. Do, then, whatever you can; be pleased, when you may, to do reverence for me to the Most Reverend and Most Illustrious Monsignor, our master. I kiss your hand.[12]

from Loreto
February 16, 1549

---

the madrigal. See *Jacobi Arcadelt Opera Omnia*, ed. A. Seay, II, 1970, p. 2, system 4, at the text "chi m'a tolto'l mio cor, chi me l'asconde."

12. Exactly a century after the writing of this letter, in 1649, a rebuttal of it was written by King John IV of Portugal (1604–56), who was a musical enthusiast and a stanch admirer of Palestrina. His letter was published under the title *Defensa de la musica moderna contra la errada opinion del Obispo Cyrillo Franco*, Lisbon, 1649, Italian version published in Venice, 1666. In this little treatise, King John takes up Cirillo's attack on the music of the modern era point by point and refutes his argument that it was inferior to that of ancient times.

READING 2

NICOLA VICENTINO †

1555

Vicentino (1511–76) spent his career mostly in the service of Cardinal Ippolito II d'Este at Ferrara and in Rome. His major work is the treatise from which this excerpt is drawn (modern facsimile reprint edited by Edward Lowinsky in the series *Documenta Musicologica*, 1959). It rep-

---

† From *L'antica musica ridotta alla moderna prattica*, Rome, 1555, Libro Quarto, Cap. XXVI, p. 84ᵛ (wrongly numbered 79ᵛ). Translated by the editor.

resents the most extensive attempt of its time to revive the diatonic, chromatic, and enharmonic genera of ancient Greek music and apply them to polyphonic music. On Vicentino as theorist and composer see Henry Kaufmann, *The Life and Works of Nicola Vicentino (1511–c. 1576)*, American Institute of Musicology, Musicological Studies and Documents No. 11, Rome, 1966, as well as Kaufmann's edition of Vicentino's compositions in the series *Corpus Mensurabilis Musicae*, No. 26.

Compositions for four voices that are settings of Masses and other Latin texts must be serious and not greatly agitated. Since Masses and psalms are church compositions, it is essential that their movement be different from that of French chansons and of madrigals and villotte. Some composers set these works in a way that upsets the entire subject of the Mass, which requires a means of movement that is grave and more filled with devotion than with worldly pleasure. Some compose a Mass upon a madrigal or upon a French chanson, or upon "La Battaglia; [1] and when such pieces are heard in church they cause everyone to laugh, for it almost seems as if the temple of the Lord had become a place for the utterance of bawdy and ridiculous texts—as if it had become a theater, in which it is permissible to perform all sorts of music of buffoons, however ridiculous and lascivious. It should not be wondered at if, in our times, music is not held in much esteem, for it has been applied to low subjects, such as balli, napoletane, villotte, and other absurd matters, against the opinion of the ancients, who used it only to sing hymns of the gods and the great deeds of men. One should certainly strive to make a great difference between a composition that is to be sung in church and one that is to be sung in the chamber, and the composer should carefully sharpen his judgment and set his compositions according to the subject and purpose of the words. . . .

1. Vicentino is almost certainly referring to Clement Jannequin's *Missa La Bataille,* based on his own program-chanson, "La Bataille de Marignan." The Mass had been published for the first time in 1532.

READING 3

FROM THE DIARY OF ANGELO MASSARELLI

[*Pope Marcellus II and the Pontifical Choir*] †
1555

On this day, Good Friday, the pope came down to witness the sacred service. Yet the music performed by the singers at the service was not fitting to the solemnity of the occasion, but rather what emerged from their concordant singing was a mood of joy. Thus it was felt that it was highly improper that these days, which ought to be conducive to the recollection of the Passion of our Lord and to the assuaging of our sins in tears, should both in voices and in music be expressive of joy, above all in the very place in which the head of the church and of the Christian domain resided. Accordingly, the pope himself, having summoned his singers around him, enjoined on them, that whatever was performed on these holy days in which the mysteries of the Passion and death of Christ were celebrated, should be sung with properly modulated voices, and should also be sung in such a way that everything could be properly heard and understood.

† This text was taken from Karl Weinmann, *Das Konzil von Trient und die Kirchenmusik*, Leipzig, 1919, p. 148, and translated for the present volume by its editor. Good Friday in the year 1555 fell on April 12—that is, within the extremely short pontificate of Marcellus II (from April 10 to April 30, 1555). Almost exactly three months prior to Good Friday, on January 13, 1555, Palestrina had been admitted to the pontifical choir. The author of this diary, Angelo Massarelli, had been the private secretary of Cardinal Marcello Cervini prior to the latter's election to the papacy. Letters from Massarelli to Cervini are preserved in Florence, Archivio di Stato, *Carte Cerviniane*, B. 23, covering the period 1543–52; and while they contain no reference to music, they do, however, provide valuable information on Cervini's interests and affairs prior to 1555.

READING 4

~~~~~

Council of Trent
Canon on Music to be Used in the Mass †
September, 1562

All things should indeed be so ordered that the Masses, whether they be celebrated with or without singing, may reach tranquilly into the ears and hearts of those who hear them, when everything is executed clearly and at the right speed. In the case of those Masses which are celebrated with singing and with organ, let nothing profane be inter-mingled, but only hymns and divine praises. The whole plan of singing in musical modes should be constituted not to give empty pleasure to the ear, but in such a way that the words be clearly understood by all, and thus the hearts of the listeners be drawn to desire of heavenly harmonies, in the contemplation of the joys of the blessed. . . . They shall also banish from church all music that contains, whether in the singing or in the organ playing, things that are lascivious or impure.

† From A. Theiner, *Acta . . . Concilii Tridentini . . .*, II (1874), p. 122; the translation appears in Gustave Reese, *Music in the Renaissance*, New York, 1954, p. 449. This canon was submitted by a committee of deputies to the entire body of the Council of Trent in September, 1562, and was approved. It formed the basis for the abbreviated and very loosely worded general ban on "worldly and impure melodies" that became an official part of the council's decrees.

READING 5
CARDINAL CARLO BORROMEO, ARCHBISHOP OF MILAN

Letters from Rome to His Vicar in Milan,
Niccolò Ormaneto †
1565

At the time of writing these letters, Cardinal Carlo Borromeo (1538–84) was papal secretary of state and effectively the most powerful figure in Italian ecclesiastical affairs after his uncle, Pope Pius IV. Borromeo had been appointed archbishop of Milan in 1560 but remained in Rome until 1565 as chief minister of papal affairs, overseeing the conclusion of the Council of Trent and conducting papal business. Here and at Milan (from 1565 until his death) Borromeo made an immense reputation for his brilliance as reformer, administrator, and leader. While Borromeo has been celebrated more for his benevolence than his intransigence, it was in relation to a Borromeo letter of 1563, calling for the death of heretics, that Lord Acton coined the phrase, "power tends to corrupt and absolute power corrupts absolutely" (Acton letter to Mandell Creighton of April 5, 1887).

From a letter of January 20, 1565:

I am pleased that you have provided our students with two good masters for the rite and the singing, the Ambrosian as well as polyphonic. Concerning this I would like you to speak to the master of the chapel there and tell him to reform the singing so that the words may be as intelligible as possible, as you know is ordered by the council. You might

---

† From the Archivio dei Barnabiti, Rome: *Di San Carlo Borromeo, Lettere di Governo,* MS, vol. I. Translated by the editor; for the original Italian texts see his monograph, *The Counter-Reformation and the Masses of Vincenzo Ruffo,* Venice, 1970, pp. 92–94; or *The Musical Quarterly,* XLIII (1957), 348–50. These letters had first been quoted and described by Charles Sylvain, a nineteenth-century biographer of Borromeo, but they were not known to music historians until 1957.

have him compose some motets and see how matters go, consulting among you as to whatever seems most expedient.[1]

From a letter of March 10, 1565:

I desire above all that the matter of the intelligible music succeed according to the hope you have given me. Therefore I would like you to order Ruffo, in my name, to compose a Mass that should be as clear as possible and send it to me here. For this purpose I send you the enclosed request to present to him.

From a letter of March 31, 1565:

I shall await Ruffo's Mass; and if Don Nicola, who favors chromatic music, should be in Milan, you can also ask him to compose one. Thus by the comparison of the work of many excellent musicians we will be better able to judge this intelligible music.

1. At this time the master of the chapel at the Duomo of Milan was Vincenzo Ruffo (c. 1510–87), who held the post from 1563 until 1572. Ruffo was a native of Verona, a highly prolific and versatile composer of madrigals and sacred music, and, from 1565 on, a devoted follower of the program for musical reform expressed in these letters. In several prefaces to later volumes of his sacred music he makes explicit reference to his having adopted the principles laid down by the Council of Trent and enjoined upon him by Cardinal Borromeo.

READING 6

Excerpt from the Diary of the Papal Chapel†
Saturday, April 28, 1565

At the request of the Most Reverend Cardinal Vitellozzi we were assembled in his residence to sing some Masses and to test whether the words

† From Biblioteca Apostolica Vaticana, Liber Punctorum Capelle . . . Diario Sistino No. 7, fol. 135ᵛ. The original text was published in incomplete form, that is, without indication of the absent singers, by G. Baini, *Memorie storico-critiche della vita e delle opere di Giovanni Pierluigi da Palestrina*, Rome, 1828, I, p. 229. It was published in its entirety by F. Haberl, *Die Cardinalskommission von 1564 und Palestrinas Missa Papae Marcelli* in *Kirchenmusikalisches Jahrbuch*, VII, 1892, p. 86, n. 2. The present translation is by the editor.

could be understood, as their Eminences desire; and the following members were marked absent:

Federicus	baiocchi 15
Petrus	baiocchi 15
Petrus Paulus	baiocchi 15
Mathias	baiocchi 15
Soto	baiocchi 15 [1]

1. A baiocco was a Roman coin of small denomination; see R. Casimiri, *I Diarii Sistini, Anno, 1535,* in *Note d'Archivio,* I (1924), p. 87, n. 2.

READING 7
GIOVANNI PIERLUIGI DA PALESTRINA

Second Book of Masses
Rome, 1567

DEDICATION

To Philip of Austria, Catholic and Invincible King:

Since the utility and pleasure afforded by the art of music is a gift of heaven greater than all human teachings, and since it is particularly valued and approved by the ancient and authoritative writings of Holy Scripture, so it appears that this art can be properly exercised upon holy and divine subjects. I, therefore, who have been engaged in this art for many years, not wholly unsuccessfully (if I may rely on the judgment of others more than on my own), have considered it my task, in accordance with the views of most serious and most religious-minded men, to bend all my knowledge, effort, and industry toward that which is the holiest and most divine of all things in the Christian religion—that is, to adorn the holy sacrifice of the Mass in a new manner.[1] I have, therefore, worked out these Masses with the greatest possible care, to do honor to the worship of almighty God, to which this gift, as small as it may be, is offered and accommodated. And these products of my spirit—not the first, but, as I hope, the more successful—I decided to dedicate to your Majesty, who have taken your own name from the tradition of the Catholic faith, and who also guard the purity of the orthodox religion most ardently, and who honor and adorn the sacred services through the works and ministrations of most excellent musicians. Accept, then, most mighty and God-fearing king, these my labors as testimony of my perpetual loyalty toward your Majesty—and accept them with that kingly greatness of spirit with which you are wont to receive such gifts. If these labors should please you, then I would consider it their greatest success if they should satisfy your judgment. If they should not please you, then nonetheless my loyal affection will not waver toward the magnanimous and noble king, whom may God, the bestower of kingdoms and giver of all good things, keep for Christendom in health and well-being as long as may be possible, and grant all good wishes of honorable men. Farewell, ornament and bulwark of all who bear the name of Christians.

Giovanni Petroaloysio Palestrina

1. Virtually the same thought is expressed by Palestrina's Roman contemporary Giovanni Animuccia (c. 1520–c. 1571) in the preface to his First Book of Masses, issued at Rome in the same year as this Second Book by Palestrina and by the same publisher (the heirs of Valerio and Aloysio Dorico, see p. 77). Animuccia had succeeded Palestrina as *magister cantorum* at the Cappella Giulia in 1555 and held this post until his death in 1571, when Palestrina took it back again. In his preface of 1567 Animuccia writes: "Being led to this by the judgment of these men, I have sought to adorn these divine prayers and praises of God in such a way that the music may disturb the hearing of the text as little as possible, but nevertheless in such a way that it may not be entirely devoid of artifice and may contribute in some degree to the listener's pleasure." Neither Palestrina nor Animuccia names the men to whom they make reference in these dedications of 1567. Palestrina's reference to a "new manner" has been taken by most writers to refer to the greater use of chordal writing in the Gloria and Credo of the *Pope Marcellus Mass,* in the service of intelligibility, than had been customary in his earlier Masses.

READING 8
GIOVANNI PIERLUIGI DA PALESTRINA

Two Letters to Guglielmo Gonzaga, Duke of Mantua
1568 and 1570

Letter of February 2, 1568: †
Most Illustrious and Most Excellent Lord:

    I am certain that my small knowledge will not be comparable to the great desire I have to be of service to your Excellency, yet it seemed to me rather better to show my insufficiency than to hide it and to be ill mannered. Since I have been ordered by so excellent a lord as yourself and by the hand of so exceptional a virtuoso as master Giaches [1] to compose the Mass that is enclosed here, I have fashioned it as I have been instructed by master Annibale Capello.[2] If in this first attempt I shall not have fulfilled the wishes of your Excellency, I beg you to inform me how you prefer it—whether short, or long, or written so that the words can be understood. I will do my best to serve you according to my ability, which I will always expend in the service of your Excellency. I kiss your most illustrious and excellent hand.

Rome, February 2, 1568
Your Excellency's most humble servant
Palestrina

    † From Knud Jeppesen, *Pierluigi da Palestrina, Herzog Guglielmo Gonzaga, und die neugefundenen Mantovaner-Messen Palestrinas,* in *Acta Musicologica,* XXV (1953), 147 f., translated for this volume by the editor. Page 148 presents a facsimile of the original letter, which can also be seen in *Die Musik in Geschichte und Gegenwart,* X (1962), cols. 689–90. The article cited here contains critical texts of ten Palestrina letters ranging from 1568 to 1584.

    1. "Master Giaches" is Giaches de Wert (c. 1535–1596), the well-known composer of madrigals and sacred music. Originally a Netherlander, Wert spent his career in Italy, at Naples, Parma, Milan, and Mantua, where he was master of music at the ducal chapel of Santa Barbara until 1582. Thereafter he was a resident of Mantua until his death. For a comprehensive portrait, see Carol MacClintock, *Giaches de Wert, Life and Works,* Rome, 1966.

    2. Annibale Capello was a Mantuan agent in Rome. Jeppesen, *Pierluigi da*

Letter of March 3, 1570: ‡
Most Excellent and Esteemed Lord and Master:

After your Excellency's virtuoso had done me the courtesy of letting me hear the motet and madrigal, he ordered me on your behalf to give my opinion freely. So I say that just as your Excellency surpasses nature in each of your endeavors, so in music you surpass those who worthily serve it as a profession. In order to study it more satisfactorily I have set the motet into score, and have observed its beautiful workmanship, far removed from the common run, and the vital impulse given to its words, according to their meaning. I have indicated certain passages in which it seems to me that if one can do with less, the harmony will sound better— such as the sixth and unison, when both parts are moving with sixth and fifth ascending and at the same time certain unisons are descending; since the imitations cause the parts to move in this way, it seems to me that because of the dense interweaving of the imitations, the words are somewhat obscured to the listeners, who do not enjoy them as in ordinary music. Needless to say, your Excellency will understand these details much better than I, but I have said this in order to obey you, and thus I will always obey you when you do me the favor to give me orders, as your affectionate and most faithful servant. And as I pray our Lord to keep your Excellency, so I humbly kiss your hand.

Rome, March 3, 1570
From your Excellency's humble and devoted servant.
Giovanni Petraloysio

Palestrina, Herzog Guglielmo Gonzaga, und die neugefundenen Mantovaner-Messen Palestrinas, 149, n. 23, describes him as "a kind of cultural attaché for the Duke [of Mantua], and apparently a personal friend of Palestrina's."

‡ From Knud Jeppesen, *Pierluigi da Palestrina, Herzog Guglielmo Gonzaga, und die neugefundenen Mantovaner-Messen Palestrinas,* 156–57. Translation by the editor. For a close interpretation of this letter, see Knud Jeppesen, *Über einen Brief Palestrinas,* in K. Weinmann, ed., *Festschrift Peter Wagner zum 60. Geburtstag . . . ,* Leipzig, 1926, pp. 100–07.

READING 9
BISHOP BERNARDINO CIRILLO

From a Letter to an Unidentified Recipient †
c. 1575

Messer Annibal:

Twenty-five years ago, when I was at the Church of our Lady in Loreto, I wrote a letter to Cavaliere Ugolino Gualteruzzi on a particular problem in sacred music that has possessed me for a long time. In this letter I suggested that he undertake to get in touch with able masters of that profession to see whether it might be possible to induce them to share my feeling on the matter—which would seem to me in this respect not wholly unreasonable—since it appeared to me that music had been subjected to abuses and had lost its way for the reasons I had indicated in that letter. The letter was published without my knowledge and has been circulating about for many years; I know that you have seen it and read it, and know to what I am referring, so that I need not tire you by repeating it. At that time I happened to come upon Cardinal Marcello Cervini, later Pope Marcellus, and I had a long discussion with him about the content of the letter. Since he seemed to be very much pleased by my discourse, he told me that on his return to Rome he would let me hear something about it, and not long afterward he sent me a Mass that conformed very closely to what I was seeking.[1]

† This letter was published by P. de Angelis, *Musica e Musicisti nell' Arcispedale di Santo Spirito in Saxia*, Rome, 1950, pp. 44–46. Only the first part of the letter is translated here by the editor. The text as given by de Angelis bears no date, but from the opening reference to Cirillo's earlier letter, it can be assigned to 1574 or 1575. The "Messer Annibal" to whom it is addressed has not been identified.

1. In his article, *Palestrina*, in *Die Musik in Geschichte und Gegenwart*, Band X, 1962, p. 684, Professor Jeppesen suggests that on chronological grounds this unidentified Mass is unlikely to have been the *Pope Marcellus Mass*. Yet this possibility cannot be entirely excluded either, since Cirillo's allusions to dates are so vague that nothing definite can be inferred from them. Writing some twenty-five years after his first

It gave me great consolation and pleasure, for it meant that my thought and purpose had been taken up and in some measure put into execution. It gave hope that gradually this style would make further advances, for in this Mass it had been shown to what degree this style conformed to the music of the church and how much it attracted good Christians to devotion . . . for those who know what purposes were served by ancient music feel an infinite displeasure when they hear the music of today. . . .

---

letter, he says that Cardinal Marcello Cervini sent him the unspecified Mass "not long afterward." If this meant a date anywhere between 1549 and 1555 (the year of Marcellus's short reign and death) it could raise interesting possibilities for speculation. At present the only visit to Loreto by Marcello Cervini that I have been able to document is one that took place in February, 1555, just before his election as Pope Marcellus II. This visit is confirmed by letters of Cervini's written during his journey from Rome to Loreto and Gubbio (of which he was bishop); Florence, Archivio di Stato, *Carte Cerviniane*, Filza 51, fol. 10, letter of February 3, 1555, from Monterosi to Cardinal Farnese; and Filza 46, fol. 112, letter of February 7, 1555, from Montefano to his brother Alessandro. Alessandro Cervini resided at Montefano, and Marcello had been born there, as he himself pointed out in a letter to the pope justifying this journey (Filza 51, fol. 23, minute of letter to the pope dated January 29, 1555). Legends had it that during this trip miracles occcrred at Loreto foretelling his election to the papacy less than two months later. A more detailed investigation of Marcello's precise movements during the years 1549–55 might shed more light on the matter; for the present it remains open whether there were other trips to Loreto during this period to which Cirillo's letter could refer. Examination of the material in the *Carte Cerviniane* for these years unfortunately failed to turn up any correspondence to or from Cirillo, or any references to music or musicians.

Reflections and Speculations (1607–1828)

READING 10
AGOSTINO AGAZZARI†

1607

. . . I shall say that, since the recent discovery of the true style of expressing the words, namely, the imitation of speech itself in the best possible manner, something which succeeds best with a single voice or with few voices, as in the modern airs of certain able men and as is now much practiced in Rome in concerted music, it is no longer necessary to make a score or tablature, but, as we have said above, a bass with its signs suffices. And if anyone objects that a bass will not suffice to play the ancient works with their many imitations, I shall reply that music of this kind is no longer in use, both because of the confusion and babel of the words, arising from the long and intricate imitations, and because it has no grace, for, with all the voices singing, one hears neither period nor sense, these being interfered with and covered up by imitations; indeed, at every moment, each voice has different words, a thing displeasing to men of competence and judgment. And on this account music would have come very near to being banished from the Holy Church by a sovereign pontiff had not Giovanni Palestrina found the remedy, showing that the fault and error lay, not with music, but with the composers, and composing in confirmation of this the mass entitled *Missa Papae*

† From a facsimile of the original 1607 edition of *Del sonare sopra il basso con tutti gli strumenti*, Milan, 1933. The translation of the entire text in Oliver Strunk, *Source Readings in Music History*, New York, 1950, is followed here in all but a few minor details.

Marcelli.[1] For this reason, although such compositions are good according to the rules of counterpoint, they are at the same time faulty according to the rules of music that is true and good, something which arises from disregarding the aim and function and good precepts of the latter, such composers wishing to stand solely on the observance of canonic treatment and imitation of the notes, not the passion and expression of the words. Indeed, many of them wrote their music first and fitted words to it afterward. For the moment, let this suffice, for it would not be to the purpose to discuss the matter at length in this place.

1. This is the earliest-known claim that the *Pope Marcellus Mass* was instrumental in saving sacred music from banishment from use in Catholic churches. The passage in Agazzari's treatise was influential in spreading the story. It was translated into German by Praetorius in his *Syntagma musicum*, III, 1619, pp. 149 f., thus initiating its circulation in Germany. And it was repeated by, among others, the Italian theorists Adriano Banchieri, *Conclusioni nel suono dell'organo*, 1609, and Agostino Pisa, *Battuta della musica*, 1611. While Pisa gives no more than a routine repetition of the tale as evidence of Palestrina's greatness, Banchieri takes special pains to assert that the particular musical value of this Mass lay in its use of consonant harmonies, which he regards as a revival of the older practice of *falso bordone*. As Banchieri writes (pp. 18 f.): "It is true that in the course of time this devout idea [i.e., the use of *falso bordone*] was abandoned by composers, when again—as Agostino Agazzari writes in his treatise on instruments—Pope Marcellus was close to banishing music from the church, had not Giovanni Palestrina shown that the fault lay with composers and not with the art of music, for on that occasion he wrote the Mass entitled *Pope Marcellus Mass*, dedicated it to Pope Paul IV [*sic*] and again introduced music using consonant intervals." Banchieri suggests that intricate fugal passages are appropriate for use in instrumental music, "as has been done by Annibale Padovano, Andrea Gabrieli, and others." On the distinction between the view of Agazzari and that of Banchieri, see Helmut Hucke, *Palestrina als Autorität und Vorbild im 17. Jahrhundert*, in *Claudio Monteverdi e il suo Tempo*, Cremona, 1968, pp. 253–55.

READING 11
LODOVICO CRESOLLIO, S.J. †

1629

Pius IV,[1] a most serious-minded pontiff of the church . . . had noticed for some time that music and singing in sacred places was very little else than an abundance of delicate diminutions and vain adornments to the words, from which no benefit of piety came forth to the listeners. He then determined to set the question of banishing sacred music from the church before the Council of Trent, and he had already mentioned his aims in meetings with various cardinals and other prelates. When word of this came to the ears of Giovanni Palestrina—who was then master of the papal singers and was gifted with great skill[2]—he quickly set himself to compose some Masses in such a way that not only should the combinations of voices and sounds be grasped and remembered by the listeners, but that all the words should be plainly and clearly understood. When the pontiff had heard these works and had seen how useful they could be for the divine service . . . he changed his mind and determined not to banish sacred music, but to maintain it. This was told by Palestrina himself to a certain member of our society, from whom I heard it.

† From *Mystagogus*, Paris, 1629, Liber III, Cap. XXVII, p. 627. Original text quoted by F. Haberl, *Die Cardinalskommission von 1564 und Palestrinas Missa Papae Marcelli*, in *Kirchenmusikalisches Jahrbuch*, VII, 1892, p. 94. Translated by the editor.

1. Pius IV (Giovanni Angelo Medici) reigned from 1559 to 1565 and undertook the first implementation of the reforms set down by the Council of Trent.

2. It is not true that Palestrina was a member of the papal choir during the reign of Pics IV. In 1555–60 he was *maestro di cappella* at San Giovanni in Laterano, and from 1561 to 1566 he held the same post at Santa Maria Maggiore.

READING 12
LELIO GUIDICCIONI

~~~~~~

From a Letter to Bishop Joseph Maria Suarez †
1637

Thus, as we said, the Tridentine fathers were gathered to consider the resolution to prohibit music in the church by decree. They were motivated, I believe, by the frivolous diminutions and ornaments used in singing, which carried music too far away from the sanctity of the divine service. The day of the session was fixed. On that day they had performed a Mass that was sent there by Giovanni Pierluigi da Palestrina by means of the legate Carpi,[1] who, taking the opposed position, argued in favor of music. The mighty energy of that eminent father, the chaste and correct style of the work combined with the sweet *concentus,* and the unanimous eagerness of the singers—all this aided and sustained the music. And consequently, having scarcely heard the sweet sounds of that most exquisite and well-ordered harmony of sounds, the fathers changed

† From Joseph Maria Suarez, *Praeneste antiqua,* Rome, 1655, p. 285. Quoted by G. Baini, *Memorie storico-critiche della vita e delle opere di Giovanni Pierluigi da Palestrina,* Rome, 1828, I, p. 190. Translated for the present volume by the editor. Lelio Guidiccioni (1570–1643) was a poet and literary man, collector of paintings, and sometime canon of Santa Maria Maggiore. He translated seven books of the *Aeneid* into Italian, and was a figure of some importance in Roman cultural circles of the early seventeenth century.

1. Cardinal Rodolfo Pio de Carpi was the recipient of the dedication of Palestrina's First Book of Motets for Four Voices (1563). Baini, *op. cit.,* I, p. 190, and F. Haberl, *Die Cardinalskommision von 1564 und Palestrinas Missa Papae Marcelli,* in *Kirchenmusikalisches Jahrbuch,* VII, 1892, p. 94, claim that Pio de Carpi was never in Trent and that consequently the tale can have had no factual basis. This point has, however, been subsequently revived by Renato Lunelli, in his article *La Polifonia nel Trentino con speciale riguardo al Concilio,* in *Il Concilio di Trento,* III, 1, 1947, p. 87. Lunelli argues that Pio de Carpi could well have sent music to Trent through the intermediacy of his friend Cardinal Cristoforo Madruzzo, bishop of Trent throughout the period 1545–60 and subsequently in Rome. At present, however, there is no documentary evidence for Lunelli's hypothesis, nor any other evidence of the performance of Palestrina's music at the Council of Trent itself.

their opinion and rescinded the decree. Music flourished, and the Palestrinian seed spread marvelously through the Christian world.

READING 13
PIETRO DELLA VALLE†

1640

As for ecclesiastical compositions, since I have embarked on the subject, I too admire that famous Mass by Palestrina that so pleases your Lordship,[1] and which was the reason that the Council of Trent did not banish music.

† From *Della musica dell'eta nostra*, 1640, in A. Solerti, *Le Origini del Melodramma*, Turin, 1903, pp. 148–79. Excerpt translated by the editor.
  1. The person addressed is Lelio Guidiccioni, author of the letter of 1637 quoted above.

READING 14
ANGELO BERARDI‡

1681

Marcellus II, because of various abuses, was determined to banish music from the church. But Palestrina valiantly defended the opposite view,

‡ From the *Ragionamenti musicali*, original edition, Bologna, 1681, Dialogo 2, p. 77. Quoted by G. Baini, *Memorie storico-critiche della vita e delle opere di Giovanni Pierluigi da Palestrina*, Rome, 1828, I, p. 176. Present translation by the editor.

showing that it was the fault of composers and not of musical learning; and on that occasion he composed the Mass that he entitled *Missa Papae Marcelli.*

READING 15
CHARLES BURNEY †

1789

Charles Burney (1726–1814), British organist and composer, is perhaps best known today for his witty and penetrating observations of the musical scene of his day, written as a result of his extensive travels all over Europe. His *General History of Music,* originally published in four volumes, 1776–89, was the first history of its kind to appear in English.

Book II of his Masses, which includes the celebrated composition entitled *Missa Papae Marcelli,* was published likewise at Rome, in 1567. Of this production it has been related by Antimo Liberati, in the letter above cited, and after him by Adami, Berardi, and other musical writers,[1] that the Pope and Conclave having been offended and scandalized at the light and injudicious manner in which the mass had been long set and performed, determined to banish Music in parts entirely from the church; but that Palestrina, during the short pontificate of Marcellus Cervini, entreated his Holiness to suspend the execution of his design till he had heard a mass composed in what, according to his ideas, was the true ecclesiastical style. His request being granted, the composition, in six parts, was performed at Easter, 1555, before the Pope and College

† From *A General History of Music,* orig. ed., III, London, 1789, pp. 189 f.

1. Burney's reference to Liberati is to Antimo Liberati, *Lettera . . . in risposta ad una del Sig. Ovidio Persapegi,* Rome, 1685, p. 23; the relevant text is quoted by G. Baini, *Memorie storico-critiche della vita e delle opere di Giovanni Pierluigi da Palestrina,* Rome, 1828, I, p. 176. The text is brief and essentially identical to that of Berardi (Reading 14, p. 32). The reference to Adami is to Adami da Bolsena, *Osservazioni per ben regolare il coro dei cantori della cappella pontificia,* Rome, 1711.

of Cardinals; who found it so grave, noble, elegant, learned, and pleasing, that Music was restored to favor, and again established in the celebration of sacred rites. This mass was afterwards printed, and dedicated to the successor of Marcellus, Pope Paul IV, by whom Palestrina was appointed Maestro di Capella to the Pontifical chapel.* [2]

* [*Author's note*]: The friends of choral music will doubtless be curious to have a faithful and minute account of a composition which had sufficient power to preserve their favorite art from disgrace and excommunication; and having before me an accurate score of it, which Signor Santarelli himself procured for me out of the Sistine Chapel, where it is still performed, I can venture to assert that it is the most simple of all Palestrina's works: no canon, inverted fugue, or complicated measures, having been attempted throughout the composition; the style is grave, the harmony pure, and by its facility the performer and hearer are equally exempted from trouble.

2. Contrary to what is asserted here, the dedication (see Reading 7, p. 22) is to King Philip II of Spain; Pope Paul IV, far from appointing Palestrina maestro of the pontifical chapel, dismissed him from membership in September, 1555. Palestrina was never again a member of the pontifical choir.

READING 16

GIUSEPPE BAINI †

1828

Despite its severe limitations, the work by Giuseppe Baini (1775–1844) ranks even now as not only the first, but still the most comprehensive, study of Palestrina, and a landmark in the field of musical biography. Its major fault lies in the discrepancy between the source material assembled by Baini (much larger than that of any predecessor) and his lack of critical thinking with which to interpret it, as is made evident through this passage. The main points in this excerpt were effectively refuted by F. Haberl, *Die Cardinalskomission von 1564 und Palestrinas Missa Papae Marcelli*, in *Kirchenmusikalisches Jahrbuch*, VII (1892), but not before Baini's account had spread widely among musicians and far beyond, in effect replacing the undocumented tale of Agazzari and later writers with

† From the *Memorie storico-critiche della vita e delle opere di Giovanni Pierluigi da Palestrina*, Rome, 1828, I, pp. 215–16 and 228–29. Translated by the editor.

this much more elaborate, but poorly documented and capricious, interpretation. The international distribution of Baini's narrative was assured
by its early translation into German by F. S. Kandler, Leipzig, 1834,
from which, as Haberl noted, it flowed into "historical volumes large and
small, articles, essays, speeches, citations, treatises, poems, and panegyrics."
Haberl's aim was to show that the Commission of Cardinals of 1564 had
an essentially disciplinary function, not a musical one, and that the manuscript evidence, as he understood it, pointed to an earlier date of composition, well before 1564–65. Since the evidence is thoroughly re-examined
in the Jeppesen article provided in this volume, it need not be reviewed
again here. Suffice it to mention that while the pendulum of scholarly
interpretation continues to swing as new evidence appears, it has little
effect on the circulation of Baini's version by those writers who know
nothing of later scholarship on the subject, but have only Baini at their
disposal, directly or indirectly. An example is Luigi Barzini, *The Italians*,
New York, 1964, pp. 307–08.

It was finally resolved, to the mutual satisfaction of Cardinal Vitellozzi
(who was very partial to the music of Palestrina) and Cardinal Borromeo,
then archpriest of Santa Maria Maggiore, of which Palestrina was
maestro at that time (Palestrina was also attached in some manner to the
college of papal singers as an ex-member)—it was resolved that Palestrina
should be given a commission to write a Mass that should be serious,
ecclesiastical, free of every admixture of the secular in its subject, melodies, and measure. . . . If Palestrina succeeded, the cardinals promised
to make no changes in the state of church music; if not, they let it be
known that the steps that would be taken would be decided by them and
the other six members of the congregation on the enforcement of the
decrees of the Council of Trent.

Cardinal Borromeo took on this commission himself. Summoning
Palestrina before him, he told him face to face to compose a Mass in the
desired manner, enjoining on him all possible effort to prevent the possibility that the pope and the Congregation of Cardinals might be en-
couraged to ban music from the apostolic chapel and from the
church. . . .

Poor Pierluigi! He was placed in the hardest straits of his career.
The fate of church music hung from his pen, and so did his own career,
at the height of his fame. . . .

* * *

On Saturday, April 28, 1565, by order of Cardinal Vitellozzi, all the
singers of the papal chapel were gathered together at his residence. Car-

dinal Borromeo was already there, together with the other six cardinals
of the papal commission. Palestrina was there as well; he handed out the
parts to the singers, and they sang the three Masses already mentioned
[the Masses *Illumina oculos meos, Benedicta es,* and the *Pope Marcellus
Mass*]. Here is the entry of the secretary of the college of singers, Cristoforo Hojeda in the manuscript diary of 1565. . . .[1]

This most eminent audience enjoyed the three Masses very much.
But the greatest and most incessant praise was given to the third, which
was extraordinarily acclaimed and, by virtue of its entirely novel character, astonished even the performers themselves. Their Eminences heaped
their congratulations on the composer, recommending to him to go on
writing in that style and to communicate it to his pupils.

1. The entire evidence for this paragraph is provided by the diary entry given
above as Reading 6 (p. 21). It is quoted by Baini in this context, but incompletely.
Baini's basis for "identifying" the three Masses listed here is simply their presence in
the MS Cappella Sistina 22 (see Jeppesen, p. 118); no other precise evidence of what
was actually sung at the trial of April, 1565, has yet come to light, though numerous
suggestions have been made. The letters of Borromeo, presented as Reading 5 (p. 20),
along with other evidence, suggest the possibility that a Mass by Ruffo could have
been among them.

THE SCORE
OF THE MASS

ACKNOWLEDGMENT

This score of the *Pope Marcellus Mass* was taken from the *Opere Complete di Giovanni Pierluigi da Palestrina* (vol. IV), edited by Raffaele Casimiri and published by L'istituto Italiano Per La Storia Della Musica, with whose permission it is here reproduced.

POPE MARCELLUS MASS

Kyrie

Gloria

Credo

Credo

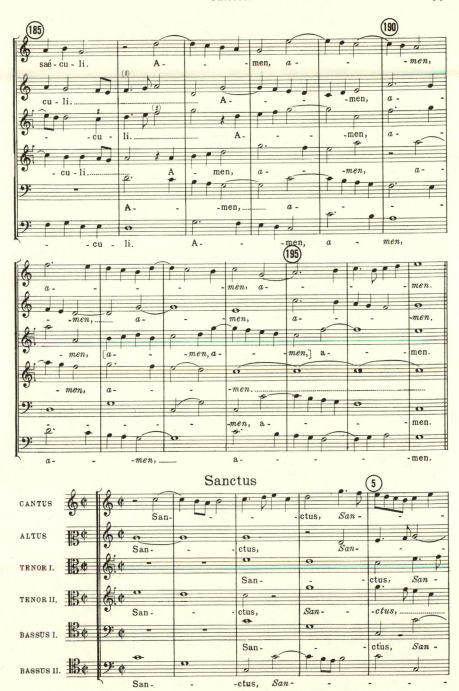

Sanctus

Benedictus

Agnus Dei I.

Agnus Dei II.
7 VOCUM

HISTORY
AND ANALYSIS

In this section, all footnotes, unless otherwise noted, are by the author.

LEWIS LOCKWOOD

～～～

Notes on the Text and Structure of the
Pope Marcellus Mass

1. SOURCES AND EDITIONS

A. Primary sources

Earliest printed source: *Joannis Petri Aloysi* [sic] *Prae/nestini Missarum Li/ber Secundus* [printer's emblem] *Cum gratia et privilegio.* [Colophon:] *Romae/Apud Haeredes Valerii et Aloysii Doricorum/fratrum Brixiensium./Anno Domini, MDLXVII.*

This first edition of the Second Book of Masses is printed in large choir-book format, in-folio. For a translation of the dedication, addressed by Palestrina to King Philip II of Spain, see Reading 7 (p. 22). Earliest manuscript sources: (1) Vatican City, Biblioteca Apostolica Vaticana, Cappella Sistina MS 22, No. 4, fols. 71^v–93; (2) Rome, Archivio di Santa Maria Maggiore, MS J. J. III, 7, fols. 1^v–22 (on deposit at the Biblioteca Vaticana).

B. Secondary sources

For a list of reprints of the 1567 edition up to the year 1600 see Knud Jeppesen, *Palestrina,* in *Die Musik in Geschichte und Gegenwart,* X, col. 663.

For a list of secondary manuscript sources see the same article by Jeppesen, col. 674. The manuscripts include a number of sources of the seventeenth, eighteenth, and nineteenth centuries that are of doubtful textual authority, if any, in comparison to the sources listed above. Of the later sixteenth-century manuscripts that contain the Mass, one that deserves further study is Modena, Archivio Capitolare, MS XII, a large choir book in several hands, containing identified works by Jaquet of Mantua and Orazio Vecchi; the *Pope Marcellus Mass* was added at the end of the manuscript in a hand distinctly different from the earlier hands in the manuscript.

C. Modern editions

Of the many modern editions of the Mass, those that deserve particular mention are the ones edited by F. Haberl, Arnold Schering, and Raffaele Casimiri, all of which differ in their editorial principles. The Haberl edition (*Palestrina Werke,* vol. XI) uses the original clefs and note values, with regular bar lines in breve measures throughout. The version edited by Arnold Schering (Eulenburg Edition, no. 963, London and Zurich, preface date 1923), uses modern clefs with note values reduced by half, and makes some use of irregular barring of the full score in the Gloria, Credo, Sanctus, and Agnus Dei I, freely alternating 2/2 and 3/2 bars; the Agnus Dei II is transcribed entirely in 3/2. The Casimiri edition (Palestrina, *Opera Omnia,* vol. IV) uses modern clefs, note values reduced by half, and regular barring throughout in semibreve measures.

The present edition uses the Casimiri score; several obvious typographical errors in early printings of that edition have now been corrected—Patrem: tenor 1, bar 48, the word "propter" was incomplete; altus, m. 51/4, an erroneous slur over c^2 has been removed; Sanctus: altus, bar 56, the half note has been corrected from g^1 to a^1.

2. PERFORMING FORCES

If we assume that the insertion in the later 1560s of the *Pope Marcellus Mass* into what became the Cappella Sistina MS 22 indicates its intended performance by the singers of the pontifical choir, it seems safe enough to take the size of that famous professional ensemble as a contemporary standard for the performance of this six-voice Mass. While the size of the pontifical choir fluctuated in the sixteenth century, it did so within ascertainable limits. Under Pope Leo X (1513–21) it had as many as thirty-six singers; in 1533, under Pope Clement VII, it was reduced to

---

1. Also valuable but now difficult to find is the edition prepared by Alfred Einstein and issued in the series *Musikalische Stundenbücher,* published by Drei Masken Verlag, Munich, 1921; for a copy of this edition I am indebted to Professor Wolfgang Osthoff. In Einstein's preface he observes that the 1598 edition of Palestrina's Second Book of Masses differs from the original edition of 1567 in a number of details of text fitting, from which Einstein concludes that the 1598 readings represent Palestrina's "last and authentic intentions." While this conclusion is the purest speculation, to be treated with extreme caution, the reader having access to the Einstein edition may well find it useful to compare its treatment of text and accidentals with those of Haberl, Schering, and Casimiri.

twenty-four (seven sopranos, seven altos, four tenors, six basses). In the period of Palestrina's first major patron, Pope Julius III (1550–55) it had twenty-eight singers; and it was later reduced to twenty-one by Sixtus V in 1586.[2] The pontifical choir was probably the only important performing group of its era that normally sang *a cappella*. The Cappella Giulia, on the other hand, had a regular organist, as did the musical establishments of other Italian churches large and small. Despite the austere preferences of some Counter Reformation prelates, other instruments were probably also used in churches from time to time, certainly in northern Italy outside Milan. In princely households and courts and in civic institutions in which music was performed, instruments of many kinds were almost certainly used to accompany singers in the performance of motets and Masses. Although the *Pope Marcellus Mass* can be effectively sung *a cappella,* it loses nothing in historical authenticity if accompanied by organ, and the discreet addition of viols and winds would be entirely appropriate, as long as the text is fully clear and the voices predominate.

3. CLEFS

The original clefs are indicated at the opening of the Kyrie I, Crucifixus, Et in Spiritum, Sanctus, Benedictus, Agnus Dei I and II. While the original sources lack names for the vocal parts, those adopted by Casimiri follow obvious implications of clef and range. In the assignments of names and staff positions to the bass parts, Schering follows Haberl, while Casimiri, following the 1567 print, shifts course midway through the score; in the Kyrie, Gloria, and Credo the two bass parts in Casimiri's edition are reversed in name (bassus 1 and bassus 2) and position, while in the Sanctus and Agnus Dei they agree with Haberl-Schering. The source of this ambiguity is the virtual identity of these parts in range and function. The editor is forced to choose between concluding the Gloria or the Credo with c in the bottom voice of the score—he cannot have both.

The combination of clefs used in this Mass—G_2, C_2, C_3, C_4—entails a relatively high tessitura for all voices when combined with the untransposed Ionian mode with C as tonal center. On the reasons for this and

2. See F. Haberl, *Die römische "schola cantorum" und die päpstlichen Kapellsänger bis zur Mitte des 16. Jahrhunderts,* in *Vierteljahrsschrift für Musikwissenschaft,* III (1887), 251–83; and Helmut Hucke, *Die Besetzung von Sopran und Alt in der Sixtinischen Kapelle,* in *Miscelánea en Homenaje a Monseñor Higinio Anglés,* Barcelona, 1958–61, I, p. 381.

the relationship of tessitura to mode, clef, and range in Palestrina's works
see Siegfried Hermelink, *Dispositiones Modorum,* Tutzing, 1960.

4. MENSURAL ORGANIZATION AND BARRING

The mensuration sign ₵, shown in the Casimiri score at the beginning of
Kyrie I and the remaining movements, is not ₵ in the modern sense but
is part of the mensural system that prevailed throughout the sixteenth
century, itself an outgrowth of a much older system. The mensuration
sign C indicates the proportional relationship of note values on two
levels: it signifies the binary division of the breve (◫) into two semibreves
(∞) and of the semibreve into two minims (♩♩); while the stroke through
the ₵ indicates that the tactus (the unit of counting by an up-and-down
movement of the hand) falls on the breve.[3] Like other mensuration signs,
it appears to have supplied only an implicit framework for the accentua-
tion of the specific rhythmic material of a given measure. I hesitate to
say that it was entirely neutral since it seems clear from Jeppesen's exhaustive studies that the controlled treatment of dissonance and con-
sonance in the music of Palestrina is based substantially on a sense of
regularly recurring "strong" and "weak" beats on minims, as it no doubt
is to some extent also in works of other composers.[4] But the patterns of
linear structure need not be regarded as being subordinate to dissonance
treatment, at least in Palestrina, and in that sense the metrical organization of a line need not be, and seldom is, a simple accent pattern of four
beats to a measure. A cardinal mistake in the performance of sixteenth-
century music is that of emphasizing the metrical accent with heavy
downbeats and light upbeats at the expense of the buoyant rhythms of
the single line.

Problems of rhythmic interpretation are partly derived from the use
of the score, an essentially heuristic device that is and was no more than
a convenient means of aligning the parts. That scores were known to
sixteenth-century musicians is clear from both surviving examples and

3. See Willi Apel, *The Notation of Polyphonic Music,* 5th rev. ed., Cambridge,
1953, p. 148, and Gustave Reese, *Music in the Renaissance,* New York, 1954, p. 180,
n. 152, citing other discussions of the tactus. For a basic introduction to the complex
network of actual and potential relationships between the tactus, the mensuration
signs, and the other notational features of early polyphony, see Arthur Mendel, *Some
Ambiguities of the Mensural System,* in H. S. Powers, ed., *Studies in Music History,*
Princeton, 1968, pp. 137–60.

4. See Knud Jeppesen, *The Style of Palestrina and the Dissonance,* 2nd ed., London, 1946.

some testimony by writers on music; [5] that Palestrina made use of them is clear from his own letter to the duke of Mantua (Reading 8, letter 2, p. 25) in which he acknowledges having received the duke's motet and says that he has set it into score "in order to study it more satisfactorily." Even though scores were known, singers rarely, if ever, used them for performance as far as we can tell; they sang from unbarred individual parts in choir books or part books. To the individual singer the most prominent rhythmic features were those that he encountered in his own part—their relationship to a regular metrical pattern was for him far less significant. Even where all voices are reduced to a single rhythmic motion, the delicate accentual configurations that emerge from the text setting frequently disagree with or overlap the bar lines. It is true that no score can reflect the elasticity and animation of sixteenth-century rhythms; [6] yet neither should a score be confused with an analysis. The performer of this work is therefore heartily invited to go through his own part and make sample rebarrings of it in accordance with the natural declamation of the text and the nature of the linear setting supplied by Palestrina. On the assumption that we can intelligently place a bar line immediately before the correctly accented syllable of a word, and especially before the most fully accented syllable within a cluster of words, we can offer the following samples:

Ex. 1 Gloria, opening measures (= Casimiri score, mm. 1–10/1, cantus)

Et in ter - ra pax ho - mi - ni - bus bo - næ vo - lun - tá - tis, Lau - da - mus te

Ex. 2 Credo (= Casimiri score, mm. 85/4–89/1)

Et re - sur - re - xit ter - ti - a di - e

Yet even in the Kyrie I, in which the syllables of the brief text cannot be distributed with much certainty, both the shape of the opening subject

5. See Edward Lowinsky, *On the Use of Scores by 16th-Century Musicians*, in *Journal of the American Musicological Society*, I (1948), 17–23; and his *Early Scores in Manuscript, ibid.*, XIII (1960), 126–73.

6. For a convenient introduction to this aspect of sixteenth-century music see Reese, *Music in the Renaissance*, p. 213, and other references in index under "rhythmic conflict among parts"; also the many arresting contributions of Otto Gombosi, including his review of Curt Sachs's *Rhythm and Tempo*, in *Journal of the American Musicological Society*, VII (1954), 221–28.

in tenor 1, cantus, and the remaining voices and the interplay of diverse rhythms can be more easily perceived in the following representation:

Ex. 3 Kyrie I: A sample rebarring of mm. 1–8 of the Casimiri score

5. ACCIDENTALS

Despite occasional misunderstandings and assumptions to the contrary, the problem of unspecified accidentals (often broadly termed *musica ficta*) is still meaningful in the late sixteenth century, and certainly for Palestrina. Indeed, his restriction of harmonic materials to an essentially diatonic vocabulary with limited use of explicit chromatic tones not only does not lessen the importance of this problem, but, on the contrary, tends to magnify it. To understand this apparent paradox we need to perceive two coexisting currents in the late sixteenth century. One attracted composers who were striving to extend the hitherto normal intervallic limits of the traditional tone system to include a wide range of chromatic tones, continuing experimental tendencies begun early in the century.[7] On the other side were composers whose work remained

---

7. See the still valuable book by Theodor Kroyer, *Die Anfänge der Chromatik im italienischen Madrigal des XVI. Jahrhunderts,* Leipzig, 1902, and the essay in reply by R. von Ficker, *Beiträge zur Chromatik des 14. bis 16. Jahrhunderts,* in *Studien zur Musikwissenschaft,* II, 1914. More recently, the most striking contributions to this field have been made by Edward Lowinsky in such studies as *The Goddess Fortuna in Music,* in *Musical Quarterly,* XXIX (1943), 45–77; *Secret Chromatic Art in the Netherlands Motet,* New York, 1946; *Adrian Willaert's Chromatic "Duo" Re-examined,* in

fundamentally within traditional concepts of the diatonic gamut and hexachord system that went back to the earlier Middle Ages, in which accidentals were thought of as additions to the system (*musica recta*) and did not alter its substance. Indeed, the very preservation of the system as a basis for musical thinking and writing implied a restricted indication of accidentals along with, one assumes, a compliant attitude about their use by performers. The business of performers was to apply them according to time-honored "rules" and with taste and sense. These "rules," as I have formulated them in a brief summary elsewhere,[8] are as follows: (1) a note above the syllable *la* is to be sung as *fa;* (2) the linear tritone and diminished fifth are, wherever possible, to be converted into perfect intervals; (3) vertical tritones and diminished fifths and octaves are, wherever possible, to be converted into perfect intervals; (4) in progressions from imperfect consonances to adjacent perfect consonances, the closer imperfect consonances are to be used (M3 $<$ P5; M6$<$P8; m3$>$unison; m6$>$P5). This rule of "propinquity" often covers situations found in cadences.[9]

One of the most useful initial tasks that the performer can carry out is that of collecting and weighing the practices of earlier editors regarding accidentals in order to uncover assumptions that they may or may not have made clear about their use of accidentals. To facilitate this for the *Pope Marcellus Mass,* a complete tabulation of the accidentals used by Haberl, Schering, and Casimiri is appended to this section.

Haberl and Casimiri follow the now commonly accepted principle of placing each "original" accidental to the left of the note affected, each editorial accidental above the note. Schering, perhaps because his edition appeared in a series otherwise devoted to classics of eighteenth- and nineteenth-century music, took the liberty of ignoring the problem altogether and set all accidentals on the staff. As if in a half gesture toward the conscientious performer, Schering put some of these accidentals in

Tijdschrift der Vereeniging voor Nederlandsche Muziekgeschiedenis, XVIII (1956), 1–36; and *Matthaeus Greiter's Fortuna: An Experiment in Chromaticism and in Musical Iconography,* in *The Musical Quarterly,* XLII (1956), 500–16, XLIII (1957), 68–85. Also Kenneth Levy, *Costeley's Chromatic Chanson,* in *Annales musicologiques,* III (1955), 167–95. The article *Musica ficta* in *Grove's Dictionary of Music and Musicians,* 6th ed. (forthcoming), will have a comprehensive bibliography on the subject.

8. See Lewis Lockwood, *A Sample Problem of Musica Ficta: Willaert's Pater Noster,* in H. S. Powers, ed., *Studies in Music History,* Princeton, 1968, p. 176.

9. For a more extended discussion of the "rules" see Edward Lowinsky, Introduction to *Musica Nova,* ed. H. Colin Slim, *Monuments of Renaissance Music,* I, Chicago, 1964, pp. viii–xxi.

parentheses, leaving others without them; but this reflects no consistent principle whatever, and not even all the accidentals in the original 1567 print are used in his edition or referred to in notes.

Parentheses are also used by Casimiri for some of his editorial accidentals, evidently to signify that these accidentals are "suggested" or "optional" while those without them are presumably more strongly recommended.

In this highly controversial domain the conscientious performer will also wish to know what the best original source would have told him, and to make this as clear as possible, the table that follows indicates not only which accidentals were used by the three earlier editors but which were explicit in the print of 1567. That this source can be provisionally taken as being closest to Palestrina's conception is an assumption based on its time and place of origin, issued as it was by the principal music publisher of Rome at this time during Palestrina's residence there and bearing a dedication by him; it could conceivably have had some form of editorial supervision by the composer.[10] The Mass in this edition contains only eight accidentals, which are listed here with an indication of their apparent purpose:

Explicit Accidentals in *Pope Marcellus Mass,* 1567 Edition

	Measure	*Accidental*	*Presumed purpose*
Et in terra			
cantus	15/1	♭	To insure a Phrygian cadence on A at m. 16
bassus 1	15/3	♭	To insure a Phrygian cadence on A at m. 16
altus	57/1	♯ (= ♮)	To provide a major third in local cadence on G
tenor 2	42/1	♯	To provide a major third on A
Patrem			
altus	58/3	♯	To insure a major third in final cadence on D
	71/1	♯ (= ♮)	To provide a major third in local cadence on G
bassus 2	64/1	♭	To insure a Phrygian cadence on A
Agnus Dei I			
altus	37/2	♯ (= ♮)	To prevent a Phrygian cadence on A

10. Evidence of careful proofreading of the Second Book of Masses is provided by two original corrections of wrong pitches (Christe, bass 1, m. 32/1, g corrected from b; and Kyrie II, bass 1, m. 61/1, c corrected from previous pitch, not visible). Both of these were made by printing single notes on small stubs of paper and gluing the stubs down to the printed page, covering the previous pitches. This was also done, of course, for the other Masses of the print where necessary; in the *Missa de Beata Virgine,* Kyrie II, altus, a stub of this type corrects nine consecutive notes. My observations are based on the copy now in Bologna, Civico Museo Bibliografico Musicale.

...ctions of the *Pope Marcellus Mass* show particular
...ain of these passages, inevitably not to all. Note, for
...e of voice exchange at "Tu solus sanctus, Tu solus
...lus Altissimus" (Gloria, mm. 93–101), and in the Credo
...the following passage (thus printed to show identity in
...ables):

> Genitum, non factum,
> Consubstantialem

..."Et unam sanctam" and the parallels that follow it (Credo,

...er striking feature of this Mass is its structural use of contrast-
...sonorities. Not only does Palestrina use diverse successive sub-
...the full ensemble for variety, but he employs them in strategic
...s that can help to shape both individual phrases and much
...nits as well. In the Gloria and Credo the manifest principle is
...either movement should begin with the full complement and
...successively alternate voice groups until the most effective moment
...e tutti is reached. In the Et in terra this moment is made to coin-
...with the repetition of the words "Domine fili," then proceeding to
...genite" and "Jesu Christe" (mm. 34–44), and even then interrupted
...n, with the tutti returning on the repetition of the name. The plan
...s follows:

	Et in terra pax hominibus	S, A, T II, B II
	bonae voluntatis	S, A, T I, B I
4	Laudamus te	S, A, T II, B II
4	Benedicimus te	S, A, T I, B I
3	Adoramus te	T I, T II, B II
4	Glorificamus te	S, A, T II, B I
5	Gratias agimus tibi	S, A, T I, T II, BII
3	propter magnam gloriam tuam	S, T II, B I
4	Domine Deus, Rex caelestis	A, T I, B I, B II
3	Deus Pater omnipotens	S, T II, B I
4	Domine Fili	S, A, T I, B II
6/5	Domine Fili/unigenite	tutti/S, A, T I, T II, B II (exchanging with B I)
5/6	Jesu Christe/(repeated)	S, A, T I, T II, B II/tutti

It is interesting to see that all of these accidentals affect cadences on secondary modal degrees (G, D, A) and that most of them render explicit the major third in these cadences. Not one is devised to avoid an awkward or "forbidden" linear interval; rather, all of them arise from harmonic situations that the individual singer could not have solved without these accidentals. From this we can derive support for the view that linear intervals subject to change through accidentals were left to the individual singer.

Careful scrutiny of the many accidentals recommended by Casimiri shows his tendency to introduce the raised leading tone at cadences (the *subsemitonium modi*) whether or not these are covered by what I have called rule 4; yet one also notes his tendency to raise only the second tone of resolution in the familiar $\frac{4}{3}$ suspension in the rhythm ♩♩♩♪♪♩ (for example, Credo, Et in Spiritum, altus, m. 177/3). Here and in parallel cases I would strongly recommend raising both tones of resolution, since the implied chromatic motion seems to me out of keeping with the function of these passages and with Palestrina's approach to linear content. The other editorial accidentals will be found to conform to one or another of the rules discussed earlier.

6. DISTRIBUTION OF TEXT

The earliest sources for this Mass are characteristic of their time in leaving it to the singer to fit syllables to notes in the Kyrie and, in large measure, in the Agnus Dei—not, however, in the Gloria and Credo. Casimiri follows the useful practice of distinguishing text drawn from the 1567 print, given in Roman type, and text assigned by him, given in italic. It should also be noticed that in the Kyrie the word "eleison" is mostly treated by Casimiri as a four-syllable word ("e-le-i-son" rather than "e-lei-son"), differing in this from Haberl and Schering and following Italian patterns of pronunciation.

7. ASPECTS OF STRUCTURE

Since the essay by Professor Jeppesen presented in this volume deals at length with the question of mode, composition type, and thematic material in the Mass, I can restrict these brief comments to several other aspects of the work.

A. Text divisions and text symmetries

In setting the invariant text of the Ordinary of the Mass, every composer could choose, within limits, his own methods of dividing its larger textual units into discrete movements. With Palestrina, the most prolific Mass composer of the century, these choices in part conform to standard procedures of the type described by Cerone (see Jeppesen, p. 106) and in part reveal his own preferences.

Of the three movements with short text, the only one having a mandatory organization is the Kyrie, which is always divided into three sections, while the Sanctus and the Agnus Dei can be treated in a variety of ways. In the Agnus Dei the number of movements that are set is the major variable. The liturgical norm calls for two Agnus Dei settings that end "miserere nobis" and a third that ends "dona nobis pacem." The composer could set a maximum of three in polyphony (with reduced complement for the second), or only two, or even one. With two or three sections the final Agnus, as here, is normally set for an expanded number of voices and is an occasion for a display of elaborate compositional technique—in this case a three-voice canon. From Josquin to Palestrina, and beyond, there is a general trend toward writing fewer than three Agnus Dei sections and toward eliminating the expanded number of voices for the last section. Josquin, as a rule, writes three sections and never less than two, a practice followed in the next generation by Willaert, Gombert, and Morales.[11] But for Palestrina, the twofold Agnus Dei is the normal type, and it is likely enough that the omission of the second Agnus Dei from the 1567 print was a practical step aimed at cutting down the bulk of the publication, not a matter of choice;[12] similar truncations of Masses had been known in Italian prints since the 1530s. Toward the end of the century the single Agnus Dei, without added voices, becomes the standard.

In the Sanctus there is greater latitude. In all his Masses Palestrina uses at least eight different ways of dividing the text, and the one chosen here—Sanctus//Hosanna//Benedictus (reduced choir)//Hosanna "ut supra" (that is, repeated)//—is not the most common. In more than

11. A fuller account of these conventions in the text divisions of the Sanctus and Agnus Dei in the sixteenth-century Mass is given in my monograph, *The Counter-Reformation and the Masses of Vincenzo Ruffo*, Venice, 1970, pp. 173–76.

12. The 1567 print is made up of exactly one hundred sheets (including title page and final page) divided into sixteen signatures of six sheets each (A$_{1-6}$ up to Q$_{1-6}$) plus a final half-signature of three sheets (R$_{1-3}$). Since the *Pope Marcellus Mass* is the last Mass in the volume, it is entirely conceivable that the decision to omit the Agnus Dei II, with its seven voice parts, was made when the volume was set up in type and its full bulk was known. In the absence of special studies of the Roman printers of this time, especially of the brothers Dorico, nothing more can now be said.

forty of his Masses he pref~
Sanctus and Pleni text~
and writing fewer but~
ences form part of a lar~
shortening the Mass sett~
plexity of its inner divisio~
polyphony in place of plain~
ment on the time needed for ~
tendencies would be entirely
Counter Reformation Europe.

In the Gloria and Credo sim~
to special external requirements, ~
of text counted most. The two-part~
and Qui tollis) constitutes the minim~
very short and telescoped Gloria setting~
shortest Mass types of the period—the so-~
is also as concise as possible, consistent ~
sonority provided by the four-voice Crucifixu~

Within the Gloria and Credo, at what~
mediate level," the most striking features of ~
handling of verbal symmetries that are built int~
the most obvious are passages in which concaten~
immediate climax—for example (Gloria, mm. 8–16).

Laudamus te
Benedicimus te
Adoramus te
Glorificamus te

It is not merely the grammatical parallel or the repetitio~
gives this passage its effect, but its steady accretion of syl~
the accented syllable: one syllable before the accent in "Laud~
in "Benedícimus" and "Adorámus," and three in "Glorificámu~
set one note to a syllable, as is often done, the declamation is b~
form a small textual-musical unit of potentially dramatic motio~
goal, and this is true whether the composer is Palestrina or Vivaldi,~
or Beethoven. Of longer span are text symmetries such as the follow~
from the Gloria (mm. 61–92):

Qui tollis . . . miserere nobis
Qui tollis . . . suscipe deprecationem nostram
Qui sedes . . . miserere nobis

88

The two long s~
attention to cer~
instance, the u~
Dominus, Tu s~
(mm. 38–42) a~
number of syll~

as well as a~
146–152).

Anoth~
ing vocal ~
groups of~
ordering~
longer ~
that n~
should~
for th~
cide ~
"un~
aga~
is a~

The Patrem similarly opens with a four-voice group, then alternates units of three, four, and five voices, reserving the full choir for the climactic and possibly symbolic phrase, "per quem omnia facta sunt" ("by whom all things are made"). In both movements special skill is devoted to gaining maximum sonorous variety in those passages, relatively rare in this "intelligible" Mass, in which there is immediate repetition of text. Aside from the ending of sections and the passage on "Domine fili" cited above, there are only three such passages in the Gloria and only six in the Credo; typically these entail not only a shift of voices but a redistribution of the same musical material in double counterpoint. An example is "Et in unum Dominum" of the Patrem, where the repetition is handled in this way

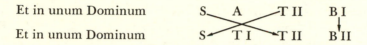

Et in unum Dominum   S   A   T II   B I

Et in unum Dominum   S   T I   T II   B II

B. Harmonic aspects

That controversies arise in the harmonic analysis of sixteenth-century music, at least by methods analogous to those of the more traditional analytic approaches to tonal music, is scarcely surprising. Yet these problems and controversies illuminate the perspectives in which music of this period is often seen, and are therefore doubly instructive; they reveal a modern tendency to emphasize contrapuntal techniques and intervallic structure (in a nonfunctional sense) but little general interest in harmonic procedure in the tonal sense. Reasons for this arise not only from doubts about the validity of this approach, but from the obvious disjunction between this "pretonal" music and the complete hierarchical range of functional harmonic means that came into being in the period of full-fledged tonality. The difficulties of this type of analysis are evident enough, yet too little has been done in this direction to warrant well-informed negative conclusions.

One valuable attempt to redress the balance in recent years is a study by Andrew C. Haigh, who raises important questions and provides new insights into Palestrina's handling of modal harmony.[13] From a

13. Andrew C. Haigh, *Modal Harmony in the Music of Palestrina*, in *Essays in Honor of Archibald T. Davison* (Cambridge, 1957), pp. 111–20; the complete data on which this article is based are found in Haigh, *The Harmony of Palestrina*, Diss., Harvard University, 1945.

substantial sampling of the harmonic content of Palestrina's works, Haigh found that the distinctions among the modes in which the works are written are not abstractly irrelevant to their harmonic content, but that to a considerable degree the individual modes possess "characteristic" harmonic tendencies. Thus, the untransposed "Ionian" tends to have, as Haigh puts it, "a numerically strong 'tonic' C and a 'dominant' G which is almost equally strong," while the " 'subdominant' F . . . is only about half as strong as the 'dominant' . . . and next in strength is the 'submediant' a (A)." This broad result is clearly applicable to the *Pope Marcellus Mass,* with its preference for initial G as harmonic point of inception for entire sections, and its even stronger predominance of C as final harmony and as modal "tonic." The co-ordinate use of G and C within this modal context has been observed by other writers, including Hermelink, with whose theories of modality and clef assignment Haigh's statistical results seem, at least in principle, entirely reconcilable.

In terms of small-scale harmonic components, Haigh observes that if the primary triadic harmonies used by Palestrina are arranged in a cycle of fifths, in the order B♭, F, C, G (g), d (D), a (A), e (E), b, there is a tendency to what he calls "modal harmonic gravitation" toward the center of the cycle. The tendency of harmonies is "toward the center of the total harmonic sphere"—that is, toward the central modal tonics. He also finds that the use of root progressions by fifths and fourths greatly exceeds that of root progressions by seconds or thirds, an observation separately confirmed for this Mass by Bobbitt.[14]

That this Mass can indeed be intelligibly approached in terms of harmonic content and progression seems intuitively clear from the strongly "chordal" content of the Gloria and Credo, in which a latent sense of harmonic direction, certainly over the span of the individual phrase, is scarcely deniable. Yet precisely owing to the narrow range of harmonic possibilities and since functional harmonic motion creating "modulation" in the later tonal sense does not yet exist, there is inevitably a sense of oscillation, of traversing the same terrain again and again. Clearly the exploration of relatively autonomous harmonic "regions" is not a part of the system of this music, which depends rather on contrasts emerging from contrapuntal and sonorous means of articulation and from the lesser variety afforded by cadences on differentiated modal degrees. Thus in the Gloria, the Phrygian cadences on A and the uses of

14. R. Bobbitt, *Harmonic Tendencies in the Missa Papae Marcelli,* in *The Music Review,* XVI (1955), 273–88.

A, d (D), and e as cadence points, with similar variety in the Credo, are significant elements of larger punctuation. Noteworthy, too, is the power-ful recurrence of plagal motion, and it is not surprising that root motion downward by fifths has been found to be the most frequent intervallic progression in the Credo.[15] This emphasis on the fourth above and the fifth below the modal "tonic" is also visible in the plagal cadences at the conclusion of almost all large sections of the Mass, but it is evident, too, in linear terms, in the formation of the very opening figure of the Mass, as first stated in tenor 1 and the cantus, most emphatically in the figure that is stated and repeated by basses 1 and 2. Here, the important aspect is not its undoubtedly accidental resemblance to the opening of the *L'homme armé* tune, but its projection of the hexachordal members *ut–fa* as a bass figure supporting the upper voices, with motion by leap from *ut* to *fa,* returning by step to *ut.* The procedure of projecting a significant interval at the beginning of a movement and of a larger work and then relating later material of the composition to it seems to me particularly important for Palestrina, and helps to account for not merely global char-acteristics of his works, but for the ordering of larger units within a composition. It helps to illuminate the sense of organic coherence con-veyed by many of his works.

C. *Means of Articulation*

In this concluding segment I want to take a more comprehensive look at one section of one movement of the Mass—the Kyrie I—as a sample problem in analysis. The problem here is to account, in some degree for the combination of elements of the work whose coexistence gives it its total form—the unfolding of the individual line, the contrapuntal net-work, the intervallic structure within the network—but beyond these, the relative function of each larger member of the whole design.

Despite the extensive use of elision and overlapping of phrase end-ings and phrase beginnings, along with the smooth flow of this poly-phonic style, a close look at Kyrie I reveals a delicate sense of proportion in the larger layout of the section. It seems to me fruitful to regard the movement as having five principal members or phrases, each of which closes with a well-articulated cadence and supplies a different combina-tion of rhythmic, linear, contrapuntal, and harmonic elements, all of them set in a certain directed order. A glimpse of this five-phrase view is given here, with the phrases indicated by Roman numerals:

15. *Ibid.,* 280.

Phrase	I	II	III	IV	V
Measures	1–4	5–8	9–14	15–18	19–24
Predominant modal center at beginning and end of phrase	G G	G C	C C	C C	C C

The basic scaffolding that supports this view is not only the articulation provided by the cadences, but the special structural roles of bass 1 and bass 2. While each is in part related motivically to the other voices, they are nevertheless much more closely related to one another through a carefully structured chain of close imitations at the unison, bordering on canon without being fully canonic. The special qualities of this pair are derived not only from the successively different lengths of their component phrases and their overlapping entrances, but even more strikingly from the changing distance of imitation between them, which can be shown as follows:

Measure		
2/1–5/3:	7 minims
5/3–9/1:	7 minims
9/1–12/1:	6 minims
15/2–16/2:	2 minims
19/2–20/4:	3 minims

It goes without saying that the phrase structure of the two lower voices reinforces the cadential articulation above them. What the table reveals is something more interesting for the shape of the movement—the gradually accelerating sense of pace arising from the changing time interval of bass 1 and bass 2. The long opening interval of seven minims used for the first two points of imitation gives scope and breadth to the opening segment. This is followed by the gradually telescoping effect of shortening the interval to six minims then reducing it drastically to two minims, followed by a slight expansion to three minims at the close. The crucial turning point in bass 1 and bass 2 is at mm. 9–10 (bass 1) and mm. 13–14 (bass 2), in which the figure is first approached from the fourth below and then from the octave below as the harmonic center shifts from G to C. This significant harmonic turning of the piece on its axis is reinforced by the balance in length and function between the two subphrases of mm. 1–4 and 5–8. Note that phrase 1 begins with the pure and modally suggestive perfect intervals—the octave d^1—d^2, to which is added its fifth below, Thus the initial G center of phrase 1 is only gradually arrived at, and there is no full G triad until, precisely, the opening of phrase 2 at m. 5. This motion to G from *its* fifth above, whether initially heard as implicit dominant moving to tonic or as tonic moving to subdominant, is then paralleled exactly in the further motion from G at m. 5 to C at m. 9, from which point onward C is solidly planted as the tonic; it has been reached by steady motion through two downward perfect fifths. (A larger sense of symmetry may be visible in the three-voice canon of the Agnus Dei II, at the other end of the Mass, which moves in exactly the reverse order—upward by fifths from G to D to A.)

If we attempt to capture even in a crude synthesis something of the combined effect of the quasi-canonic bass parts, together with the harmonic and cadential articulation of the phrases and the contrapuntal treatment of the successive points of imitation, we can glimpse something of the whole while inevitably leaving many details to further study and more extensive analysis. The attempt follows in the chart on p. 94.

Phrase	I	II	III	IV	
Measures	1–4	5–8	9–14	15–18	19–24
	Exposition (16 minims)		Middle section (12 minims) A	Middle section (8 minims) B	Coda (12 minims)

Freely imitative exposition in upper voices plus B II at close time interval, leading to entrance of T II and B I at m. 5 and phrase 2. Subject in exact imitation in B I and B II. Initial implication of D leads to G, confirmed by cadence at m. 5/1 and first full triad on G, then to C with cadence at m. 9. In cantus, linear apex g^2 and lower extreme $f(\sharp)^1$ reached in mm. 3–4, providing maximum linear activity at beginning of the movement.

B I and B II subject extended to 12 minims and imitative time interval shortened to 6 minims. Parallelism and voice exchange in upper voices in mm. 10–12 and 13–15. Repeated *ut–fa–mi* figure in cantus elaborates the opening subject's contour.

B I and B II have intensified imitation at interval of 2 minims. Closely spaced motion in quarter notes in all voices. Imitation between T I and cantus at 2 minims joined to that of B I and B II.

Slight expansion of B I and B II time interval to 3 minims. Closing figures in all voices leading to final plagal cadence.

94

Accidentals in Editions of the Pope Marcellus Mass

In this table the Casimiri edition is used as the standard of comparison. Accidentals not otherwise marked are located *above* the notes affected. The accidentals found in the 1567 edition (there always as adjacent accidentals, of course) are shown here with the abbreviated designation, "orig." The designation of the two lowest voices in the Mass follows Casimiri's labeling throughout.

		Casimiri	Schering	Haberl
Kyrie I				
C	4/4	sharp	sharp	sharp
A	8/2	sharp	—	—
Christe				
B II	29/3	sharp	sharp	sharp
	30/2	sharp	sharp	sharp
Kyrie II				
C	68/4	sharp	—	—
Et in terra				
C	15/1	flat (orig.)	flat	flat
	41/2	sharp	sharp	sharp
A	4/4	sharp	sharp	sharp
	27/4	sharp	sharp	sharp
	37/2	sharp	sharp	sharp
	48/2	sharp	sharp	sharp
	53/3	sharp	—	—
	57/1	sharp (orig.)	—	sharp
		(= natural)		(= natural)
T I	11/3	sharp	sharp	sharp
	38/4	sharp	sharp	sharp
	45/1	sharp	—	—
T II	3/3	sharp	—	—
	9/3	sharp	sharp	sharp
	16/1	sharp	sharp	sharp
	40/4	sharp	sharp	sharp
	42/1	sharp (orig.)	sharp	sharp
	56/3	sharp	sharp	sharp
B I	15/3	flat (orig.)	flat	flat
	28/3	sharp	sharp	sharp
	30/3	sharp	—	—
B II	43/3	sharp	sharp	sharp
Qui tollis				
C	94/2	sharp	—	—
	95/1	sharp	sharp	—
	96/3	sharp	—	—
	97/4	sharp	sharp	sharp
A	68/2	sharp	—	sharp
T I	66/2	sharp	sharp	sharp

		Casimiri	Schering	Haberl
	78/3	sharp	sharp	sharp
	100/4	sharp	sharp	sharp
	110/2	sharp	—	—
T II	65/2	flat	—	—
	81/3	sharp	sharp	sharp
	116/4	sharp	—	—
B I	63/2	sharp	sharp	sharp
	96/2	sharp	—	—
	96/4	natural	—	—
B II	99/2	sharp	—	—
Patrem				
C	52/4	sharp	sharp (52/3)	sharp (52/3)
	63/4	sharp	—	—
	64/3	sharp	sharp	—
A	4/4	sharp	—	—
	7/2	sharp	sharp	sharp
	15/4	sharp	sharp	sharp
	22/2	sharp	sharp	sharp
	27/2	sharp	sharp	sharp
	32/2	sharp	sharp	—
	40/2	sharp	sharp	—
	55/2	sharp	sharp	sharp
	57/1	flat	—	—
	58/3	sharp (orig.)	sharp (58/2)	sharp (58/2 and 58/3)
	63/3	flat	flat	flat
	67/3	sharp	sharp (67/2)	sharp (67/2)
	71/1	sharp (orig.)	—	sharp (70/2) sharp (71/1)
T I	12/3	sharp	—	—
	13/2	sharp	sharp	sharp
	18/2	sharp	sharp	—
	21/4	flat	—	—
	30/4	sharp	—	—
	51/1	sharp	sharp (Schering has misprint e here)	sharp
	57/4	sharp	sharp	sharp
T II	33/4	sharp	sharp	—
	49/4	sharp	sharp	sharp
	54/3	flat	—	—
	57/1	flat	—	—
B I	20/4	flat	—	—
	53/4	flat	—	—
B II	56/2	flat	—	—
	64/1	flat (orig.)	flat	flat

		Casimiri	Schering	Haberl
Crucifixus				
C	78/2	sharp	—	sharp
	83/3	flat	—	—
	88/4	sharp	sharp	sharp
	101/2	flat	—	—
	114/4	sharp	sharp	sharp
A	78/1	sharp	sharp	sharp
	78/3	sharp	—	sharp
	80/4	sharp	sharp	sharp
	111/2	sharp	—	—
	112/2	sharp	—	—
T I	84/1	sharp	sharp	sharp
B	99/2	flat	—	—
	113/4	sharp	—	—
Et in spiritum				
C	180/4	sharp	sharp	sharp
A	131/2	sharp	sharp	sharp
	148/4	sharp	sharp	sharp
	152/4	sharp	sharp	sharp
	158/4	flat	flat	flat
	177/3	sharp	sharp (177/2)	sharp (177/2)
	180/1	flat	—	—
	186/1	sharp	—	—
T I	159/2	sharp	sharp	sharp
	185/4	sharp	sharp	sharp
	186/3	sharp	—	—
T II	164/3	sharp	sharp (164/2)	sharp
	181/4	sharp	sharp	sharp
B II	176/1	flat	flat	flat
Sanctus				
C	13/4	sharp	sharp	sharp
	45/4	sharp	sharp	sharp
A	13/1	flat	—	—
	15/4	sharp	sharp	sharp
	26/4	sharp	sharp	sharp
	49/4	sharp	—	—
T II	55/1	flat	—	—
B I	51/4	sharp	sharp	sharp
B II	15/1	sharp	—	—
	26/2	flat	—	—
	48/4	sharp	—	—
Hosanna				
C	66/1	sharp	—	—
	67/3	sharp	—	—
T I	66/4	sharp	sharp	sharp
T II	62/1	sharp	—	—

		Casimiri	Schering	Haberl
	63/3	sharp	sharp (63/2)	sharp (63/2)
Benedictus				
C	20/2	sharp	—	—
	24/4	sharp	sharp	sharp
A	5/1	sharp	—	—
	9/2	flat	—	—
	14/4	sharp	sharp	sharp
T I	2/1	sharp	—	—
	8/3	sharp	—	—
				sharp (36/4)
	37/1	sharp	sharp	sharp (37/1)
T II	12/3	sharp	—	sharp
	23/4	sharp	—	—
Agnus Dei I				
C	9/3	sharp	—	sharp (9/2)
	18/4	sharp	—	—
A	6/4	sharp	sharp	sharp
	12/4	sharp	sharp	sharp
	27/1	sharp	—	sharp
	27/4	sharp	sharp	— (implied?)
	37/2	sharp (orig.) (= natural)	—	sharp
	38/2	sharp	sharp	sharp
T I	6/1	sharp	sharp (equivalent of Casimiri 5/4)	sharp (5/4 and 6/1)
	12/1	sharp	sharp	sharp
	40/2	sharp	sharp	sharp
	44/4	sharp	—	—
	48/1	sharp	—	—
T II	10/3	sharp	sharp	sharp (10/2)
	44/1	sharp	—	—
	48/4	sharp	—	—
B I	37/2	sharp	—	—
Agnus Dei II				
C I	8/1	sharp	—	—
	23/2	sharp	sharp	sharp
	33/4	sharp	sharp	sharp (33/3)
	35/4	sharp	—	—
A I	3/4	sharp	—	—
	10/2	sharp	—	sharp
	15/4	sharp	sharp	sharp
	27/4	sharp	sharp	sharp
	42/4	sharp	sharp	sharp
A II	32/3	sharp	—	—
T	48/3	flat	—	—
B II	21/2	sharp	—	—

KNUD JEPPESEN

Problems of the Pope Marcellus Mass:
Some Remarks on the Missa Papae Marcelli
by Giovanni Pierluigi da Palestrina †

Knud Jeppesen (1892–1974) was one of the most distinguished figures in
twentieth-century historical musicology, recognized especially for his
significant contributions to the study of music of the Renaissance. He
was long active as lecturer on music history and theory at the Royal
Conservatory in Copenhagen and as professor at the University of Aarhus,
combining these activities with those of organist and composer. A founder-
member of the International Musicological Society, he was editor of its
journal, *Acta Musicologica,* for many years (1931–54). His principal publications include scholarly editions of music of the fifteenth, sixteenth, and
seventeenth centuries, among them *Der Kopenhagen Chansonnier* (1927);
Die mehrstimmige italienische Lauda um 1500 (1935); *La Flora* (1949); *Le
Messe di Mantova* (Palestrina, *Opere Complete,* vols. XVIII–XIX [1954])
and *Italia Sacra Musica,* 3 vols. (1962). His extended monographs, apart
from articles in scholarly journals, include an influential study of dissonance in the music of Palestrina, originally published in Danish in 1923,
subsequently in German (1925), and in English as *The Style of Palestrina
and the Dissonance* (1927; 2nd ed., 1946). His most recent major work is
La Frottola, 3 vols. (1969–70).

Although Palestrina's *Pope Marcellus Mass* is perhaps the best-known
and most widely discussed work in the earlier history of music, some of
the most important aspects of the composition remain largely unex-
plored. This is especially true of its mode, its composition type, its
thematic material, and its date of origin. These remarks represent an
attempt to clarify each of these aspects of this work.

† The second part of this essay, dealing with the sources and dating of the Mass,
originally appeared separately under the title *Wann entstand die Marcellus-Messe?,*
in *Studien zur Musikgeschichte: Festschrift für Guido Adler,* Vienna, 1930, pp. 126–36.
The entire essay was published in *Acta Musicologica,* XVI–XVII (1944–45), 11–38. The
present translation is by the editor.

I. MODE

In the later sixteenth century, the theory of polyphonic mode was comparatively antiquated in relation to contemporary practice, and it was therefore poorly suited to reflect the musical realities of the time. Closely connected to this is the fact that musicians continued to grant recognition only to the formulas of the monophonic Gregorian modes, even though in this period these modes had lost all their earlier practical significance. Even after the twelve-mode theory had been formulated quite authoritatively by Glareanus (1547)—the most important innovation in the modal doctrines of the sixteenth century—the medieval system remained otherwise intact: the mode of a polyphonic piece was determined almost exclusively by the range and melodic activity of the tenor—that is, according to purely melodic criteria.

But as the entire course of the development of music in the sixteenth and seventeenth centuries was toward harmonic stability and tonal centralization, the unreliability of the older modal system became increasingly apparent, and efforts were made to revise and strengthen the theory of mode. This is closely bound up with the gradual rise of the typically Baroque fugal imitation at the fifth. Owing to this development, it became increasingly common to regard not only the end, but the beginning of a composition as having a determining role in its modal designation.

Symptomatic in this connection is a discussion of Palestrina's Mass *Panis quem ego dabo* that took place in the mid-seventeenth century. In an anonymous tract of 1654 [1] the question of the modal assignment of this Mass is raised, and the answer that is given is that it belongs to the second mode (Hypodorian) because its tenor (*rector et guida tonorum*) extends from A to a and employs d as tonal center. The question is then posed—and this is the new and remarkable feature of the discussion—how this modal assignment can be reconciled with the fact that in the imitative opening of the Mass the voices begin on c and g. The answer is somewhat naïve, but otherwise plausible: "This is a procedure often followed by older musicians, who did so because the Gregorian melodies begin on the second, third, fourth, fifth, sixth, and seventh degrees of the tone or mode in which they are written." Thus this divergence is justified by reference to the old practice of beginning on a tone other

---

1. See G. Baini, *Memorie storico-critiche della vita e delle opere di Giovanni Pierluigi da Palestrina*, II, Rome, 1828, p. 360.

than the tonic or dominant, as often happened also in plainsong. Other theorists give more imaginative discussions of this and other discrepancies, which must have seemed highly unusual to seventeenth-century musicians imbued with a unified view of tonality. Among them the Roman theorist Pier Francesco Valentini (c. 1586–c. 1652) merits special mention.

Valentini, particularly in his treatise entitled *Duplitonio,* presents a substantially new theory of the church modes. He proceeds from the observation that in works by sixteenth-century masters, especially Palestrina, the imitative openings of compositions are formed not only by tonic and dominant but also quite regularly by tonic and subdominant. The division of the octave by the fifth he calls the "harmonic" division (using a then familiar term borrowed from ancient mathematics); the division by the fourth he calls the "arithmetic." Then he divides each of Glareanus's twelve modes into two forms: a harmonic and an arithmetic.[2] Thus the first "harmonic" mode has as range and principal tones D–A–D; the first "arithmetic" mode, on the other hand, has the principal tones D–G–D; the second (plagal) "harmonic" has A–D–A, and the corresponding "arithmetic" plagal mode has A–D–A, and the corresponding "arithmetic" plagal mode has G–D–G, and so forth.

According to Valentini, not only the beginnings of compositions, but their internal cadences are determined by these divisions of the octave by fourth and fifth, and Valentini attributes this division of the modes to plainsong as well. Dr. Lucas Kunz, after careful study of this last aspect of Valentini's theory, finds that it is not borne out in practice. On the other hand, he finds Valentini's system to be "particularly well adapted to a detailed modal classification of the polyphonic music of his own and earlier periods."

In my view this is not quite true. But in order to clarify the question, it will be necessary to consider briefly the treatment of mode in the works of Palestrina, whose compositions occupy a central position in Valentini's discussion as well.

How Palestrina conceived the modes from a theoretical standpoint is difficult to determine. He seems never to have expressed himself directly on the matter, and from the titles of his works, such as the Masses labeled *Primi toni, Quinti toni* and *Octavi toni,* and also the Magnificats in the eight modes, it can only be seen that he accepted the traditional eight

---

2. See the useful study by P. Lucas Kunz, *Die Tonartenlehre des römischen Theoretikers und Komponisten Pier Francesco Valentini,* Kassel, 1937.

modes of plainsong. But if we examine his treatment of mode in practice, as revealed in his works, it is clear, first of all, that in addition to the traditional eight modes he recognized the tones added by Glareanus (the Ionian and Aeolian); second, that there is a substantial difference between his treatment of mode and the modal principles of plainsong. This raises in turn the problem of the authentic-plagal distinction.

Although this distinction was actually obsolete as soon as one departed from plainsong, it remained in a kind of artificial intellectual preservation down to our own time. Almost all theorists held fast to it, no matter what their relationship to the medieval system of musical theory.[3] Even in the Palestrina complete edition, F. X. Harberl used both concepts to establish the modes of the Masses.

Nevertheless, a study of Palestrina's works makes it quite clear that for him there was no difference in the treatment of authentic or plagal mode.

In general there are in Palestrina's usage only five modes: Dorian, Phrygian, Mixolydian, Aeolian, and Ionian. He uses the Lydian modes (modes 5 and 6) either with a signature flat (in which case they are no longer Lydian but F-Ionian),[4] with an Aeolian ending, or as C-Ionian (see the Magnificats of volume XXVII, pp. 20, 26, 58, 63, 113, 121, 191, 202, 251).

Of particular interest on this question are the views of the well-known Modenese theorist and composer Giovanni Maria Bononcini, in his *Musico prattico*. He hails the traditional twelve-mode theory (pp. 116 ff.) but notes that each four-voice composition is a composite of two modes, so that if the tenor is authentic the bass is plagal, and vice versa. Nevertheless he holds fast to the traditional means of modal designation—that is, by means of the tenor. But since he does not appear to be wholly satisfied with this, he adds, evidently on his own account, a few more means of making this distinction, of which he says: "the authentic has the characteristic of tending toward the higher region, and the plagal toward the lower" (p. 118). What he means by this is seen from the musical examples he gives (of his own composition), twelve imitative duos in all, one for each mode. Here the themes of the authentic modes tend to emphasize

3. A rare exception is Johann Joseph Fux, who, although he largely reckons with twelve modes, considers the plagal modes to be largely superfluous in practice. See *Gradus ad Parnassum*, German ed., 1742, p. 164.

4. The only exceptions to this in the entire thirty-three volumes of the Palestrina *Werke* are two short pieces in the Second Book of Madrigals for Four Voices (vol. XXVII, nos. 24, 25), which, although they are liberally sprinkled with accidental B♭'s, must be construed as being in the Lydian mode.

upward motion, while the plagal themes tend to move downward. These, however, are tendencies that have no validity in the general practice of the sixteenth century, and even Bononcini remarks that this rule is probably arbitrary, but that "by observing it one will proceed according to their nature" (that is, the nature of the modes).

Although Bononcini recognizes twelve modes in all, in a practical sense he reckons only with seven: Dorian, Hypodorian, Hypomixolydian, Aeolian, Hypoaeolian, Ionian, and Hypoionian. He thus excludes Mixolydian as well as Phrygian and Lydian (in both forms). Aeolian is used instead of Phrygian and Hypophrygian, Ionian instead of Lydian and Hypolydian, and Aeolian instead of Mixolydian!

In this connection it should be noted that Mixolydian is one of the dominating modes of the sixteenth century,[5] and Bononcini's view that it may be replaced by Aeolian, or that it is replaceable at all, is incomprehensible to me. On the other hand, when Bononcini argues that this is also true for Phrygian, one can follow his argument, since Phrygian compositions of the sixteenth and seventeenth centuries often—indeed most frequently—begin with imitations on e and a (in short, are really Aeolian compositions). Finally, the replacement of Lydian by Ionian, as mentioned earlier, agrees entirely with the practice of the Palestrina period.

As is well known, the decisive point for the tonality of a composition is the conclusion. This was so in plainsong [6] and it remained so in later centuries. The beginning of a composition, on the other hand, was much more freely handled, and one finds, not least in the sixteenth century, that a great number of pieces begin tonally in quite a different manner than they conclude.

The *Pope Marcellus Mass* is a famous example of this divergence. In this work the relationship between beginnings and endings of sections is as follows:

Kyrie I begins with an imitation on d and g (that is, Mixolydian)

5. In Palestrina the mode most frequently encountered is the Dorian; then follow, in almost equal proportions, Ionian and Mixolydian; finally (both much more sparingly used), Aeolian and Phrygian.

6. Guido of Arezzo, *Micrologus*, chap. 11: "While every melody is made up of all tones and intervals, the tone that ends the melody is the most important, and it is therefore sung as a held tone that dies away. The tones leading up to it so adapt themselves to this final tone that in a wonderful way they seem to take from it their color and physiognomy. . . . When the last tone of a melody is sung, we recognize

but after eight measures it moves to C (Ionian) and remains there to the end. The Christe begins in Ionian with three voices and closes on G (a semicadence, such as often occurs in Christe sections and at the conclusion of the first part of a motet in two sections).

Kyrie II begins in imitation on d and g and closes in Ionian. The Gloria begins with a four-voice G-major harmony and ends on C. The Credo resembles the Gloria, while the Sanctus begins and ends on C. Agnus I resembles Kyrie I; Agnus II begins with a G-major triad and ends in Ionian.

The Mass thus fluctuates between the Mixolydian and Ionian modes, and so it is hardly surprising to find that there is some uncertainty about its mode. According to Baini (*op. cit.*, I, p. 228) it belongs to the eighth mode (Hypomixolydian); Haberl, too, designates it as Mixolydian (PalW XI, p. viii), though less definitely. In more recent times it has been regarded as Ionian.[7]

In order to shed some light on the relationship between the beginning and ending of a composition and its modal assignment, I have sought to trace these features through the entire contents of the Palestrina *Complete Works* edition.[8] Proceeding on the assumption that the concluding harmony is actually the tonic, one finds that there are four general types of opening formulas:

A. The first notes of the imitation are the tonic and its dominant (in optional order).

B. The first notes of the imitation are the tonic and the fourth above or fifth below (in optional order).

C. The first notes of the imitation are the dominant note and the fifth above or fourth below it (in optional order).

D. The first notes of the imitation are the third above the tonic and the fifth above or fourth below it (in optional order).

The results are as follows:

---

the mode clearly from what has preceded. At the beginning of a melody, however, you do not know what will follow; but at the end you perceive at once what has come before. Thus it is the final tone to which we must attend most carefully."

7. See, for example, Wilhelm Widmann, *Sechstimmigen Messen Palestrinas*, in *Kirchenmusikalisches Jahrbuch*, 1930, p. 95: "The mode is Ionian, but with a frequent mixture of Mixolydian"; also J. Samson, *Palestrina*, 1939, p. 58: "If this is not C major, nothing is."

8. I have indicated only compositions that begin with imitation (and not restricting these to compositions beginning with imitation at unison or octave). For the two-section motets I have counted both sections, and in the Masses, Kyrie I, Christe, Kyrie II, Gloria, Credo, Sanctus, and Agnus I (as well as Agnus Dei II and III, if set).

	Scale degrees			
	A (1 and 5)	B (1 and 4)	C (5 and 5)	D (3 and 7)
Dorian	207	18 a	44 f	29 j
Phrygian	21	54 b	0	2 k
Mixolydian	121	60 c	10 g	——
Aeolian	73	34 d	4 h	6 l
Ionian	141	48 e	25 i	1 m
Total	563	214	83	38

a Cf., for example, PalW IV, p. 118; b PalW I, p. 83; c PalW I, p. 101; d PalW II, p. 148; e PalW V, p. 57; f PalW XIX, p. 36; g PalW X, p. 57; h PalW V, p. 74; i PalW II, p. 37; j PalW XXIV, p. 3; k PalW VIII, p. 98; l PalW VIII, p. 161; m PalW VIII, p. 138.

This table shows, with perhaps surprising clarity, that in Palestrina's works there is absolutely no inherent assumption that a composition shall begin with the root and fifth degrees of the tonic harmony. Still, with the exception of Phrygian, this is by far the most common procedure. But the root and fifth of the subdominant triad (to use modern terminology) and also the dominant and the modal relative harmony also appear frequently at the beginnings of compositions.

The use of the subdominant (which Valentini considered the hallmark of the arithmetic mode) is particularly prominent in the Phrygian mode, where it occurs more than twice as often as the degrees 1 and 5. This no doubt hangs together with the difficulty of handling b♮ because of its relationship to f. For the same reason, the opening formula 5–5 is not used in Phrygian and is used only sparingly in Aeolian. It is less clear, however, why the formula 1–4 is so infrequent in Dorian. This is somewhat balanced by the formulas 5–5, and 3–7, which occur frequently only in this mode.

In the theoretical writing of the period one finds little on this subject. Vicentino says that one can begin with unison, fourth, and fifth, etc.,

and one should not use the interval of the second, the minor or major sixth, the seventh, or the ninth; the only exception is in the second section of a composition, where these poor intervals may be tolerated because the ending of the first section will have led the singer's ear to be prepared to accept any sort of bad interval.[9]

9. Nicola Vicentino, *L'antica musica ridotta alla moderna prattica*, 1555, fol. 78ᵛ. Vicentino is thinking of cases in which the first part of a motet ends with a semi-

Almost the same thing is taught by Orazio Tigrini,[10] and also by Zarlino,
who regards as permissible opening intervals not only the unison, fourth,
and fifth, but also the third degree above the final.[11] Particularly noteworthy in this respect is Domenico Pietro Cerone, who in his *Melopeo*
(1613, p. 723) argues that owing to problems of intonation one should
strive to take care that the first notes of the various imitating voices should
stand in a consonant relationship to one another. Only in a canon or a
very strict imitative passage should one deviate from this procedure.
Cerone writes further:

> But I must warn the reader that, in a case not governed by the strict
> relationship of a canon, Palestrina used a similar principle in the motet
> *Parce mihi, Domine,* published in the first book of his motets for five
> voices. Here the first note of the superius forms a fourth with the contralto
> and quinta, a seventh with the tenor, and an eleventh with the bass. This
> may be allowed by virtue of the text, which seems to evoke a beginning of
> this kind, and by means of the setting it almost appears that the composer
> is asking pardon for his violation of normal procedures, saying to musicians,
> "Parce mihi, Domine," I have sinned against art.

The passage to which Cerone refers is the opening of Palestrina's
five-voice motet on this text (PalW IV, p. 112), reproduced below. The
situation visible here is not entirely unusual in Palestrina—namely,
that in a single passage imitations may begin at the fifth as well as the
fourth degree from the final. Although this procedure does not seem to
have been recognized by the theorists,[12] it appears fairly often in practice,
and without the textual association mentioned by Cerone; for instance,
as in Example 2 on p. 108.

This simultaneous occurrence of characteristic elements of the so-

---

cadence or with a deceptive cadence, as frequently happens, preparing the listener's
ear for a free treatment of the mode.

10. *Compendio della musica,* 1588, p. 37.

11. See G. Zarlino, *Opere,* 1589, p. 412.

12. See, for example, Cesare Crivellati, *Discorsi musicali,* Viterbo, 1624, p. 188: "If
the voices begin together in the cantilena, one should take care that they begin with
perfect consonances; if they begin with an imitation, one after the other, they may
begin with imperfect consonances but not with dissonances. The parts at the beginning
should not employ the intervals of both fourth and fifth, although in imitation it is
not incorrect to begin at the distance of a fourth from the final." (That is, although
one can make an imitation at the fourth from the final, both fourth and fifth should
not be mingled in the same imitative passage.)

Ex. 1

called "harmonic" and "arithmetic" modes suffices alone to undermine this classification. Thus it seems that Valentini's observation that the internal cadences ought to agree with the opening either in the "harmonic" or "arithmetic" formulations fails to hold true.[13] Finally, a perusal of volume IV of the *Werke* (*Liber quartus ex canticis canticorum,* 1584)

13. To add a pair of specific examples, the five-voice motet *Orietur stella* (PalW IV, p. 118) is Dorian and begins with the "arithmetic" division, but in the later course of the composition shows no further cadence on g (fourth above the tonic); the same is true of the motet *Duo ubera tua* (PalW IV, p. 71), which has no cadences on B♭ although it begins with the "arithmetic" division of the F-Ionian mode.

Ex. 2 Palestrina, motet: *Surrexit pastor bonus;* [14] mode: F-Ionian; source: PalW
V, p. 177

shows clearly that Palestrina himself did not reckon on this division of
the modes. From a close study of this collection of five-voice settings of
the Song of Songs, it appears that its contents are arranged according to
mode (it is thus a kind of *tonarium*) in that the first ten pieces are in
Dorian, the next eight Mixolydian, and so forth:

			Type					Type
1.	G-Dorian	1, 5	(A)	15.	Mixolydian	1, 4	(B)
2.	G-Dorian	1, 5	(A)	16.	Mixolydian	1, 4	(B)
3.	G-Dorian	1, 5	(A)	17.	Mixolydian	1, 4	(B)
4.	G-Dorian	5, 5 ^{2}	(C)	18.	Mixolydian	1, 4	(B)
5.	G-Dorian	5, 5 ^{2}	(C)	19.	Aeolian	1, 5	(A)
6.	G-Dorian	1, 5, 5 ^{2}		20.	Phrygian	1, 4	(B)
7.	G-Dorian	1, 5	(A)	21.	Phrygian	1, 4	(B)
8.	G-Dorian	3, 7	(D)	22.	Phrygian	1, 4	(B)
9.	G-Dorian	1, 5	(A)	23.	Phrygian	1, 4	(B)
10.	G-Dorian	5, 5 ^{2}	(C)	24.	Phrygian	1, 4, 7	
11.	Mixolydian	1, 5	(A)	25.	F-Ionian	1, 5	(A)
12.	Mixolydian			26.	F-Ionian	1, 4	(B)
13.	Mixolydian	1, 5	(A)	27.	F-Ionian	1, 5	(A)
14.	Mixolydian			28.	F-Ionian	1, 5, 5 ^{2}	(C)
				29.	F-Ionian	1, 5	(A)

14. See PalW I, p. 118; II, p. 50; VII, pp. 88, 153; IX, p. 185; X, pp. 133, 149; XI,
p. 39; XII, p. 116; XIII, p. 61; XIV, pp. 11, 16, 64, 85; XV, pp. 60, 113; XVIII, pp. 15,
31, 40, 65, 89, 91; XX, pp. 46, 53; XXIII, p. 69; XXVIII, pp. 39, 52, 92, 195; XXIX,
pp. 103, 113, 137; XXXII, pp. 13, 41, 143.

Since, as we see, the examples in Dorian of types A, C, and D are set next to one another indiscriminately, Palestrina must have regarded these forms as being essentially the same. The same situation obtains in Ionian, where instances of types A, B, and C are intermingled. From this it is clear that Palestrina considered these various forms from the standpoint of a single mode. This is particularly important because the *Pope Marcellus Mass* is an example of type C, and accordingly there can be no doubt that its modality, despite the Mixolydian color of its opening measures, can be and should be regarded as Ionian.

Further evidence for this view is supplied by the Kyrie II of the six-voice Mass *Quinti toni:* [15]

Ex. 3

Here the mode is F-Ionian with a Mixolydian beginning. It is all the more significant that Palestrina designates the composition as belonging to the fifth mode (that is, as transposed Ionian) because the piece—not only in modal treatment, but even in thematic material—resembles the well-known opening of the *Pope Marcellus Mass* to a very striking degree. The resemblance can hardly be coincidental. Still further support is lent by the fact that the *Missa Quinti toni* seems also to be very close to the *Pope Marcellus Mass* in its composition type, as will be seen.

II. THE POPE MARCELLUS MASS: COMPOSITION TYPE
AND THEMATIC MATERIAL

In 1914 Michel Brenet remarked on the Masses of Palestrina:

Since the traditions of the period required that they all be composed upon given melodies, one can feel sure that the *Pope Marcellus Mass* had as its

15. PalW XIX, p. 87. See also Agnus II, *ibid.,* p. 107.

subject either a plainsong melody, a chanson theme, or a fragment borrowed from a polyphonic composition, sacred or secular.[16]

In the years since this observation was made it has been possible to discover antecedents for the greater number of the Palestrina Masses, but not for the *Pope Marcellus Mass*. Various views have been advanced on the matter, especially in recent years.[17]

The first question is whether the work really has any antecedent at all. Brenet seems to have overlooked the fact that a good many sixteenth-century Masses are "free" compositions, works based on thematic material devised directly by the composer for the individual Mass. Cerone, who of all theorists of the period wrote most extensively on the musical treatment of the Mass, has this to say:

> The Ordinary of the Mass should be composed upon the basis of a motet, madrigal, or chanson, even one written by another composer. And thus it shall then take its title from the words that are sung to the motet, madrigal, or chanson, as follows: "Missa Virtute magna"; "Missa Vestiva i colli"; "Missa En espoir." If then the composer does not wish to make use of the aforementioned antecedents, but prefers to use instead a new invention, formulating it himself, he can entitle the Mass in this way: "Missa Sine nomine"; or, if it is short, "Missa Brevis" or "Missa L'hora e tarda." . . . And if it should be composed upon the species of any tone, it should be given the name of the tone to which the species belong; thus, *Missa Primi toni, Missa Secundi toni,* etc. But if the Mass is based upon plainsong melodies, it should be named after the plainsong, thus: *Missa De Beata Virgine, Missa Apostolorum, Missa Dominicalis, Missa Ecce sacerdos magnus, Missa Ad coenam Agni providi.*[18]

Following Cerone, then, one may conclude that a Mass that bears a title derived from neither a Gregorian melody nor from a chanson, motet, or madrigal is constructed upon themes newly invented by the composer (I would call it a "free" Mass in contrast to an "elaboration" Mass). But as is well known, this is not always the case. If we look through Palestrina's works we find four so-called "Sine nomine" Masses (PalW X, XI, XV,

16. *Palestrina,* p. 169.

17. Thus Félix Raugel, *Palestrina,* Paris, 1930, p. 77, says that "the main motives of the *Pope Marcellus Mass* are closely related to the plainsong Kyrie *Lux et origo* and *Conditor omnium,* to the 'Laudamus te' of the Gloria of Mass XV, and to the most widespread version of the *Ite missa est.*" Less convincing is the view of J. Samson, *op. cit.,* p. 176, who believes that the themes of the *Pope Marcellus Mass* are derived from the famous chanson *L'homme armé.* This thesis is entirely implausible, as will be seen. Elsewhere Samson himself observes with prudent impartiality, that "certain writers are prepared to say 'it is now proven that Palestrina borrowed the themes of the *Pope Marcellus Mass* from the *L'homme armé* melody.' 'Proven' is exaggerated; still I am inclined to say that the idea may be given serious credence."

18. For a translation of the entire section of Cerone's Book XII that bears on Mass composition and on the settings of other musical categories, see O. Strunk, *Source*

quite different type. In the first of these, the opening motive of the Mass is only slightly reflected at the beginning of the Gloria and appears elsewhere only in modified form in the Sanctus. The latter, on the other hand, makes a more extended use of the opening motive, quoting it at several places, including the beginning of the Sanctus (in somewhat modified form) and at the Agnus I in inversion. The Mass *Ad fugam* is perhaps the most artfully contrived of all Palestrina's works. Its double and triple canons extending through entire sections exclude its having a model. All the thematic material required for these special contrapuntal tasks had to be devised especially for this purpose. Still, we do perceive in this work a main motive that stands at the beginning of the Mass and then appears, in somewhat altered form, in the Sanctus and Agnus I.

The *Missa brevis* is also a freely composed Mass. This is very clear, despite Baini's assertion (*Memorie,* I, p. 363) that it is based on Claude Goudimel's Mass *Audi filia,* a statement that has been uncritically repeated to this day. In fact there is only the most tenuous and incidental resemblance between the two Masses. Apart from the opening theme, which in Goudimel's Mass is

Ex. 4

Ky - rie e - ley-son,   Ky-rie e - ley - - son

and in Palestrina's is

Ex. 5

Ky - rie e - lei - - - - - son____

and which have their first three notes in common, there is nothing else to support Baini's assertion. On the other hand there are numerous dissimilarities, principally that the Mass *Audi filia* is a "transcription" Mass in which the main motive appears in all the major divisions, while in the *Missa brevis,* as mentioned earlier, it appears only in the Sanctus in altered form.

made after this essay had been written, that the *Missa Sine nomine* (No. 36) is actually based on a six-voice motet now known in two sources: Rome, Biblioteca Santa Cecilia, MS G. 792–795, No. 48, with text "Cantabo domine"; and Augsburg, Stadtbibliothek MS 18, with the title *Beata dei genitrix.* He also suggested that the *Missa Secunda* may be based on the four-voice motet *Veni sancte spiritus,* published in PalW XXXII, p. 37, as an *opus dubium. Editor*]

The Masses *Secunda* and *Quinti toni* are notable in that none of their five major divisions begins in the same way. Yet these Masses seem not entirely without thematic connections; in the *Secunda,* the Sanctus and Agnus II begin with the same themes; in the *Quinti toni,* so do the Kyrie II and Agnus II.

On the whole it appears as though in freely composed Masses Palestrina created a certain degree of unity through thematic similarities within individual movements. The great difference between the freely composed Masses and the "transcription" Masses is that the latter are primarily organized by means of the same musical material running through all parts of the Ordinary, while the other type exhibits complete thematic freedom. In the one case the material is *per piacere;* in the other it is *obbligo.* For the "transcription" Masses the result is that in all main divisions of the Mass not only is the opening theme used, but a full elaboration of the most important themese of the model is pursued especially in the longer Gloria and Credo. In the "transcription" Masses a single appearance of a subject is rare; in the free Masses it is common. From this standpoint the *Pope Marcellus Mass* is evidently a free Mass.

The opening theme is repeated, in modified form, in Agnus I and II, and is found otherwise only in bass 2 at the beginning of the Credo. Apart from this no theme of the Mass appears more than once. That this opening subject is Palestrina's own invention is further confirmed by its striking similarity to other themes that one finds in his works. This was mentioned earlier in connection with the Mass *Quinti toni* and is especially noteworthy in the eight-voice motet *Domine in virtute tua* (PalW II, p. 153):

Ex. 6

Compare the opening of the motet with the opening of the Mass:

Ex. 7

It is immediately clear that the cantus and bassus of the two compositions are virtually identical. Doubtless the motet passage is a citation from the Mass. The Mass was published in the Second Book of Masses of 1567, dedicated to King Philip II of Spain; it was probably well received by the kings since Palestrina dedicated his Third Book of Masses of 1570 to him as well. Thus it is understandable that Palestrina should seek to offer the king a pleasant remembrance in this motet which was also written for Philip II.[24]

But there are other passages in Palestrina's works in which one finds themes strikingly similar to the *Pope Marcellus Mass* motive, although they certainly cannot be quotations:

Ex. 8

24. On August 12, 1570, Don Annibale Capello, musical agent for Duke Guglielmo Gonzaga, wrote from Tivoli (where Palestrina was then living in the Villa d'Este as master of the chapel of Cardinal Ippolito II d'Este of Ferrara) that he would soon send to Mantua a motet for eight voices, *Domine in virtute tua*, which Palestrina had written for the king of Spain. The composition was then dispatched on September 2. See F. X. Haberl, *Das Archiv der Gonzaga in Mantua*, in *Kirchenmusikalisches Jahrbuch*, 1886, p. 36.

A. Motet: *Vox dilecti;* B. Offertory: *Justitiae domini;* C. Offertory: *Sanctificavit Moyses;* D–E. *Missa L'homme armé,* Kyrie I; F. *Missa Nigra sum,* Credo; G. *Missa Nasce la gioia mia,* Gloria; H. *Ibid.,* Credo; I. *Missa Hodie Christus natus est,* Sanctus; J. *Missa Benedicta,* Credo.

The similarity between example 8D and the *Pope Marcellus Mass* motive is the basis for J. Samson's suggestion that the Mass is a disguised "L'Homme armé" Mass. Although this view is incorrect, it is understandable as an assertion about the main theme of the Mass. But when Samson submits that the second segment of the chanson melody

Ex. 9

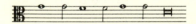

is the model for the Christe of the *Pope Marcellus Mass*

Ex. 10

as well as that the Kyrie II of the Mass is motivically derived from the chanson (*op. cit.,* p. 177), this seems to me to be utterly unconvincing.

In fact, quite a different thematic connection is involved here. A comparison of the *Pope Marcellus Mass* with the Mass *Benedicta* (PalW X, p. 80) discloses the surprising fact that the main motive of the Christe of the *Pope Marcellus Mass* is derived from the Gloria of the *Missa Bene-*

dicta. This can surely not be an accidental resemblance, but is rather a direct borrowing—and one that is, so far as I know, unprecedented in Palestrina's works. Palestrina based a number of his Masses on his own motets or madrigals, but it is not known if he ever used material from one Mass in another Mass. Here no doubt seems possible. The *Pope Marcellus Mass* passage is

Ex. 11

The passage from the Gloria of the *Missa Benedicta* is

Ex. 12

This thematic relationship suffices alone to show that the theory advanced by Samson and other writers—that the *Pope Marcellus Mass* was based on a specific, thorough-going model—is to be abandoned, as will already have been seen from the earlier discussion of the categorization of the *Pope Marcellus Mass* as a "free" Mass.

III. CHRONOLOGY

A considerable number of theorists and writers on music of the seventeenth and eighteenth centuries—the earliest, Agostino Agazzari and Banchieri, writing in 1609—declare that polyphonic church music was threatened with abolition by a pope (some say by Marcellus II, others Pius IV). Palestrina is then supposed to have changed the pope's attitude by means of the *Pope Marcellus Mass* and thus to have saved church music.

The first to occupy himself with these legendary accounts was Giuseppe Baini, the founder of Palestrina research. Baini observed that Marcellus II, in his papal reign of only three weeks' duration (of which he was active for only ten days), could scarcely have had time to concern himself with a reform of sacred music. Baini also considered it improbable, as some older writers had held, that the Council of Trent, which for some time had taken an aggressive position on sacred polyphony, should finally have contented itself with a few general and mild decrees on the subject. Baini blithely announced instead that the *Pope Marcellus Mass,* together with two other Masses by Palestrina, was written in 1565 and exerted a powerful effect on the Commission of Cardinals, who were charged with the practical realization of the council's decrees; accordingly Palestrina was named papal composer.

The sources for this so-called "three-Mass fable" of Baini's are these: (1) the diary entry made by the scribe of the papal chapel Hojeda, according to which the singers were assembled in the home of Cardinal Vitellozzi on April 28, 1565, to permit judgment as to "whether the words can be understood, as their Reverences desire"; (2) the Codex 22 of the archive of the papal chapel, which contains the three Palestrina Masses *Benedicta es, Illumina oculos meos,* and *Papae Marcelli,* and from which it can be shown that the Mass *Benedicta* was entered in 1565; (3) the fact that Palestrina's stipend as papal singer was raised beginning in June, 1565, "because of various compositions which he has had copied and are to be copied for the benefit of the said chapel." Baini accordingly dates the *Pope Marcellus Mass* in 1565.

On this point, however, Baini's theory was subjected to devastating criticism by F. X. Haberl, the second great figure in Palestrina research. In Haberl's valuable essay, *Die Kardinalskommission von 1564 und Palestrinas Missa Papae Marcelli,* in *Kirchenmusikalisches Jahrbuch,* 1892, he reports on a renewed study of Codex 22 of the papal archive, and finds that it is not a unified manuscript, written about 1565, as Baini had supposed, but consists of six different fascicles that were only brought together much later—Haberl believes in the eighteenth century. Haberl also called attention to the fact that the Mass *Benedicta,* which is found in Codex 22 (and, according to Baini, was written in 1565 together with the Mass *Illumina oculos meos* and the *Pope Marcellus Mass*), is also found in Mus. MS 46 of the Munich State Library, and that it must have been copied into that manuscript before 1562, since the manuscript was written by the copyist working under Ludwig Daser, who was succeeded in that year by Orlando di Lasso as Bavarian court chapel master.[25]

Haberl also adds this:

> The oldest source for the *Pope Marcellus Mass* is not the manuscript of the Sistine archive, but Codex 18 (in large folio) of the musical archive of Santa Maria Maggiore, which was entirely unknown to Baini. The Masses Nos. 3 and 4 of the Sistine MS 22 must surely have been copied from this manuscript,[26] which also lacks indication of title and author, for the handwriting of MS 18 of Santa Maria Maggiore is older than that of the three Palestrina fascicles of MS 22 of the Sistine archive. Only in these two MS volumes does one find the second Agnus Dei of the *Pope Marcellus Mass,* which was omitted in the printed version of 1567 (Second Book of Masses).

On the dating of the *Pope Marcellus Mass* Haberl writes:

> The date of composition must fall in the year 1554 or 1555, since Palestrina had dedicated his First Book of Masses (1554) to Pope Julius III, and had been taken into the papal chapel by him.[27]

Essentially the same view as that of Haberl was adopted by Karl Weinmann, Haberl's successor; [28] but Weinmann was able to shore up the assumptions in Haberl's arguments by reference to more recent research. For instance, the Austrian church historian Ludwig von Pastor, in his *History of the Popes* (German ed., vol. VI, 1913, p. 345), called attention to an important passage in Massarelli's diary. Angelo Massarelli, who was personally close to Pope Marcellus II and had left a detailed account of his life, reports that on Good Friday, April 12, 1555 (the third day of his pontificate), Pope Marcellus II called the papal singers together after the service and instructed them to take care that in the future the music of Good Friday services should be more in keeping with the solemn character of the day; he also set down the requirement that the music should

---

25. Daser's permission to depart was first granted, however, on May 29, 1563. See A. Sandberger, *Beiträge zur Geschichte der Bayerischen Hofkapelle* I, p. 44.

26. Haberl refers here to the Palestrina Mass *Benedicta* and the *Pope Marcellus Mass.*

27. Preface to the edition of the *Pope Marcellus Mass* in Proske's *Musica divina,* Annus II, Tomus I, Fasc. VII.

28. *Das Konzil von Trient und die Kirchenmusik,* Leipzig, 1919.

be performed in such a way that the words should be as intelligible as possible. Weinmann is doubtless correct when he connects this event (in which Palestrina participated as papal singer) with the title of the *Pope Marcellus Mass,* which is otherwise difficult to understand.

Important, too, for this problem is the interesting exchange of music and letters between Rome and Munich about 1560, which was described by Otto Ursprung.[29] With the music-loving cardinal of Augsburg, Otto Truchsess von Waldburg, acting as intermediary, compositions by Orlando di Lasso were sent to the Roman cardinals Vitelli and Borromeo, who were equally interested in music. In exchange, on January 14, 1562, there was sent to Munich "ain neuwe Mess, welche ain singer auss der Bapst. Capell so der Rossetto genant Componiert wirt guet geacht" ("a new Mass, which was written by a singer in the papal chapel named Rossetto, is well regarded"); and on November 8, 1562, "ain mess, die der Capell Maister zu Sta Maria maggior dise tag gemacht und hie fir gutt geacht wirtt" ("a Mass that was written in the past few days by the chapel master at Santa Maria Maggiore, and is highly regarded here"). There is no reasonable basis for contradicting Ursprung's assumption that the Mass by Rossetto is the six-voice Mass *Ultimi miei sospiri,* by "il Rosso," which is found in MS 45 of the old Munich court chapel collection; and that the "Mass by the chapel master of Santa Maria Maggiore" is the six-voice Mass *Benedicta* by Palestrina (Palestrina was chapel master at Santa Maria Maggiore 1561–67), which is found in Munich MS 46, a source closely connected to Munich MS 45. Both Masses are also copied into the Sistina MS 22, which is approximately contemporary with the Munich manuscripts, and the Mass *Benedicta* is the only Palestrina composition of the period 1560–70 that is included in the very important and well-preserved Munich choir books. So one can assign the Mass *Benedicta* wtih confidence to 1562, as both Ursprung and Weinmann had done.

Weinmann, however, puts the origins of the *Pope Marcellus Mass* still earlier; he notes that in Santa Maria Maggiore MS 18 the *Pope Marcellus Mass* stands first, while the *Benedicta* is entered only later, and infers from this that the *Pope Marcellus Mass* was copied earlier than the *Benedicta,* which on the basis of the Rome-Munich exchange he assigns to 1562. Weinmann summarizes the situation this way:

> We have established from the sources these chronological limits for the composition of the *Pope Marcellus Mass:* 1554 and 1563. The earlier limit is 1554 because the Mass is not found in Palestrina's First Book of Masses,

29. O. Ursprung, *Jacobus de Kerle,* Munich, 1913, pp. 12 ff.

published in this year; 1563, because the Mass is already copied by this year into Santa Maria Maggiore MS 18. The probable date of origin would seem to be 1555, in connection with the events of the pontificate and death of Pope Marcellus II.[30]

Thus the *Pope Marcellus Mass* would date from 1555, the Mass *Benedicta* from 1563. But this seems unacceptable on musical grounds.[31]

It is certainly striking that in previous discussions of the dating of the *Pope Marcellus Mass* no style-critical arguments have been advanced. And yet a rapid glance at the musical structure of the two Masses suffices to show convincingly that the *Pope Marcellus Mass,* written in the developed "Palestrina style," cannot be earlier than the Mass *Benedicta,* which exhibits archaic features. Indeed, one can say with confidence that if this were truly the case, the entire style-critical method would lose its efficacy. But before I come to these questions of musical technique, I should like to deal with the oldest sources for the *Pope Marcellus Mass* on the basis of a renewed personal study of these sources.

Codex 22 of the Cappella Sistina archive is a large choir book, consisting of 143 paper leaves, 48 cm. by 64.5 cm., with area of writing largely of the dimensions 34 cm. by 54 cm. The manuscript was written with an ink of high acid content that in the course of time has eaten its way through the paper; in 1724 (under Pope Benedict XIII) the manuscript was "restored"—that is, rebound. About 1890 the manuscript was subjected to a thorough restoration, in which the leaves were covered with transparent paper. But unfortunately the new surface was covered with a lime preparation made with wax, with the result that the wax crystallized and the pages became covered with a brownish glaze, rendering the manuscript difficult to read or to photograph as it now stands.

The manuscript shows the fine and characteristic hand of the famous scribe of the papal chapel, Johannes Parvus. Parvus was a cleric from Senlis in France, who from about 1540 to about 1580 seems to have written the greater number of the sacred music manuscripts for use in Rome. The name Parvus is found in the account books of the papal chapel for the first time on March 19, 1540,[32] but MS 18 of the Sistine

30. *Op. cit.,* p. 154. Here Weinmann avers that the *Pope Marcellus Mass* was entered into the manuscript in 1563, but on p. 140 of his book he says that in 1562 it was already copied into the manuscript of Santa Maria Maggiore.

31. The Haberl-Weinmann dating was criticized earlier by Otto Ursprung, in his preface to the Kerle volume of the *Denkmäler der Tonkunst in Bayern,* 1926, but from a different standpoint than the present one.

32. Rome, Archivio di Stato, Mandatis 868, fol. 302ᵛ.

archive can be attributed to him and dates from 1538–39. The last preserved manuscript done by him for the papal chapel is MS 21, of 1576.
Only a portion of the Parvus manuscripts of the archive were recognized
as such by Haberl in his catalogue of the papal chapel archive, and in
summary the following manuscripts are partially or entirely in Parvus's
hand: Cappella Sistina MSS 13, 17, 18, 19, 20, 21, 22, 24, 38, 39, 57, 64,
154, and 155. Haberl's view of Codex 22 (shared by Weinmann), that it
consists of six separate fascicles first brought together at the restoration in
1724, is seen on closer inspection to be incorrect for these reasons: (1)
The manuscript is written throughout in Parvus's hand, and is paginated
throughout by him. (2) It is regularly constructed in tripartite gatherings.
From the eighteenth gathering on (fol. 103), the organization into gatherings is difficult to determine because the manuscript is very tightly
bound and the paper is very pliable, but even here the system of tripartite gatherings seems to be continued, with the exception of the eighteenth
gathering (to which two leaves are pasted at the end) and the twenty-third
gathering, which is fourfold and ends with an added leaf. (3) None of
the six Masses of the manuscript starts (naturally with the exception of
the first Mass) at the beginning of a gathering. Thus, the second Mass
starts on the second page of the fourth gathering, the third Mass on the
last page of the seventh, and so forth.

It can scarcely be doubted, therefore, that the manuscript was pro-
duced by its scribe as a whole. What is surprising, then, is that while
Parvus entered the date "1568" in the capital *O* of the Osanna of the
Mass by Robledo, in the Palestrina Mass *Benedicta* that follows, the date
"1565" is entered into the *Q* of the Qui ex Patre.[33] This is explained
easily, however, by the observation that originally the material of the
manuscript was written on individual leaves, which were first glued together as pairs when the manuscript was assembled and then organized
into gatherings. The format of the pages is inherently so important, that
it must have been uncomfortable for the scribe, while writing, to have a
double folio before him to work upon. This method of writing is not
unusual for Parvus; it was the customary practice in the writing of the
older Cappella Sistina manuscripts. In the spring of 1929 I had an opportunity to observe the restoration of Sistina MS 63 (written around 1500),

---

33. Haberl says, surprisingly, that Baini had claimed that this date had been entered into the *Pope Marcellus Mass*—and Weinmann, in particular, maintains this
error. But Haberl simply misunderstood Baini, as can be readily seen by checking
Baini's *Palestrina*, I, p. 231, where the matter is set forth quite correctly.

during which the manuscript was divided into its gatherings. As with many other Vatican manuscripts, the tight binding of the manuscript made it difficult to tell in any other way that the gatherings were each made up of two leaves stuck together. Now one might perhaps suppose that the manuscript was cut apart and then glued together at the time of a later restoration; but MS 63 shows no signs whatever of a later restoration, and here and there within it one sees paper of different types mixed together in a single gathering (for instance, fols. 36–37, 35–38), which also happens in other Sistine manuscripts (for instance, in the Parvus MS 38, fol. 129–30) and shows clearly too that the scribe had worked with individual leaves at first.

The origins of MS 22 can thus be described as follows. Around 1565 Parvus had copied a series of Masses that were then circulating in Roman musical circles, and later (around 1570) he brought six of these Masses into a single volume, as follows: (1) The five-voice Mass *En douleur et tristesse* by the Belgian Noel Baudouin; (2) the five-voice Mass by the Spaniard Robledo, untitled; (3) Palestrina's six-voice Mass *Benedicta;* (4) the *Pope Marcellus Mass,* for six voices; (5) Palestrina's six-voice Mass *Illumina oculos meos;* (6) the six-voice Mass *Ultimi miei sospiri,* by Il Rosso. The Masses are thus brought together in order of number of voices —first those with fewer voices, then those with more. This is a familiar practice that Parvus also used in other manuscript volumes of Masses that still exist in the Vatican Library,[34] and that often occurs as well in the Mass prints of the sixteenth century—for example, in Palestrina's prints. This principle explains why Parvus set the Robledo Mass, copied in 1568, *before* the six-voice Mass *Benedicta,* copied in 1565.

In summary, then, this much can be said about MS 22: Haberl's theory that it is an accidental assemblage of fascicles is without foundation. But on the other hand, Baini's view that the manuscript as a whole has a close connection with the reform movement initiated by the Council of Trent is equally unsupported by the evidence. A close examination of the musical content of the manuscript shows that only in the case of the *Pope Marcellus Mass* (and perhaps, but in any event in a far weaker degree, in the Robledo Mass) can one speak of particular attention to intelligibility of text. The Mass by Baudouin, on the other hand, is

---

34. Cappella Sistina Codices 39, 154, and 155. In Codex 39 we find first two four-voice Masses, then a five-voice Mass, and finally three for six voices. In Codex 154 three four-voice Masses are followed by one for six voices; in Codex 155 two four-voice Masses are succeeded by two for five voices.

richly adorned with canons, and, except for the *Pope Marcellus Mass,* the Palestrina Masses of the manuscript belong to a pre-Tridentine phase. MS 22 is therefore emphatically not a "reform manuscript" (as Ursprung thought), but simply a collection of five-voice and six-voice Masses, which Parvus assembled in Rome about 1565–70 for the Sistine archive and which, like all other Sistine manuscripts, gives us an idea of what was "well regarded" in Roman musical circles of its time (even, as in this case, during a period of "reform").

Let us now turn to MS 18 of the musical archive of Santa Maria Maggiore, to which Haberl attributed so much importance and which he thought to contain the earliest extant version of the *Pope Marcellus Mass.* It is a large sixteenth-century choir book in brown leather binding, of 139 paper leaves, 38 cm. by 51 cm., with a writing area of about 27 cm. by 41.5 cm.; seventeen gatherings of four leaves each (the last leaf of the eighteenth double gathering is torn off). The writing shows the hand of Parvus quite clearly, and thus the origin of the manuscript was probably the Sistine manuscript. Nothing about this manuscript indicates that it is earlier than the Sistine MS 22; on the contrary, its paper shows that it is a later source.

The types of paper that Parvus used for his choir books exhibit great consistency and continuity, and offer useful criteria for the dating of the manuscripts. The paper employed by the Cappella Sistina scribe is evidently from a limited number of well-established workshops, so that the types of paper in use changed very seldom. Parvus used in all of his manuscripts only four different types of paper, all Italian in origin; and while one does not find precisely these papers represented in C. M. Briquet's *Les Filigranes* (which is based mainly on archival records in any event), one finds, nevertheless, papers that are closely related to these. The earliest type used by Parvus is very similar to Briquet's No. 493 (dated 1524–30 on the basis of documents in the archive at Udine). It was used very sparingly by Parvus—indeed only in the Sistine MSS 17 and 19, which were prepared under Pope Paul III (1534–49). Evidently this paper was left to Parvus by his predecessor, since one finds it in use in manuscripts of about 1505 to 1535.[35] The only two papers that Parvus uses in greater profusion—let us call them A and B—have a similar watermark, namely two crossed arrows, one of which is flanked by a lance ending in a star. The watermark of A is somewhat smaller than that of B, and in A the

---

35. Thus in Codex 26, written under Leo X, (1513–21); in Codex 42, written about 1507; and in Codices 45 and 55, which are adorned with the arms of Clement VII (1523–34).

arrowheads are slightly rounded off to a leaf shape, while in B they are more nearly heart-shaped.[36] The oldest Parvus manuscripts are written on paper A, at first with some admixture of paper left over by his predecessor. Written entirely on paper A are the following manuscripts: 13, 18 (1538–39), 20, 24 (1545), and 155. In MS 154 (written under Julius III, 1550–55) paper B appears for the first time; and from about 1563 on, paper A is replaced by paper B. Purely made up of B is Codex 39 (written about 1563), MS 22 (as indicated, from about 1570), and MS 57 (in part by Parvus, written about 1571). In Parvus's last manuscript for the Sistine Chapel, MS 21 of about 1576, the paper is still mainly type B, but with occasional use of a new paper, bearing a watermark consisting of a crown below a star.[37] This paper was used regularly thereafter for the Sistine manuscripts, as is shown by MSS 29 and 30, copied by Luca Orfeo about 1590–94. This last paper was also used for the manuscript of Santa Maria Maggiore, as copied by Parvus; accordingly it can be assumed that it was made around 1580, and all the evidence thus shows that the oldest known source for the *Pope Marcellus Mass* is not the Santa Maria Maggiore manuscript but Sistine MS 22 or the printed edition of 1567. This means, too, that the study of the physical properties of the sources yields no precise results on the dating of the work. Let us turn, then, as a last resort to style-critical investigation.

Any survey of Palestrina's Mass output shows the difficulty of putting his Masses in chronological order on the basis of stylistic criteria.

Three Masses, however, show a clear set of tendencies in common— namely the six-voice Mass *Benedicta es,* the *Pope Marcellus Mass,* and the Mass *Ut re mi fa sol la.* As the following remarks will show, all of these works belong to the same period of Palestrina's development, the years 1562–63. At this time Palestrina had published, of his sacred music, only the First Book of Masses in 1554. That volume had contained four Masses for four voices and one for five voices. Of the four-voice Masses the first, *Ecce sacerdos magnus,* is a strict *cantus firmus* Mass of the Netherlands type; the other three are "transcription" Masses based on motets by Andreas de Silva and Verdelot, while the five-voice Mass *Ad coenam agni providi* is built upon a Gregorian hymn melody.

The Mass *Ut re mi fa sol la,* which was first published in Palestrina's

36. B is most nearly similar to Briquet No. 6291, a paper that was used for a document of 1561–62 in the Archivio di Stato in Rome.

37. This paper is most closely related to Briquet No. 4835 (Rome, 1567–68) and Likhatscheff, *La Signification paleographique des Filigranes,* St. Petersburg, 1899, No. 3639 (Italy, 1577).

Third Book of Masses of 1570, is already present in Sistine MS 39, where the scribe, Parvus, inserted the date 1562 into the initial letter of the Patrem. It is based on the use of the hexachord as *cantus firmus,* in rhythmically varied forms, in the alto and thus follows a principle of composition that was quite outmoded by the middle of the sixteenth century.

The Mass *Benedicta es* was based, as indicated earlier, on the six-voice motet of this title by Josquin des Prez.[38] The *Pope Marcellus Mass* has, as we have seen, no evident antecedent and, apart from the Mass *Ad fugam,* can be regarded as the earliest Mass by Palestrina that is based on freely invented material.

An important "archaic" trait in Palestrina is the use of the so-called "extended cambiata": [39]

Ex. 13

This old-fashioned formula is found frequently only in his First Book of Masses. As early as the First Book of Motets for Four Voices (1563) it is quite rare; in the Second Book of Masses (1567) it is still rarer; and elsewhere—apart from a completely isolated use of it—appears only in the six-voice Mass *Ave Maria,* which doubtless belongs to the earliest of Palestrina's works,[40] and also in the above-mentioned Mass *Benedicta.*[41] Of these three six-voice Masses the *Benedicta* makes the definite impression of being the earliest. This emerges from the use of symmetrical and repeated rhythmic patterns, in the manner of old Netherlands composers, and through the use of melodic patterns repeating the same intervallic boundaries—for example:

Ex. 14

Chri - - ste___ e - - - - le - - - - i - son,

38. The motet by Josquin is, in turn, based on a liturgical Sequence melody.

39. I coined this term in my book, *The Style of Palestrina and the Dissonance,* German ed., Leipzig, 1925; the terminology is to be taken more nearly morphologically than genetically, since the classical "cambiata" must be understood as a concentrated form of the "extended" one.

40. See the preface to PalW XV.

41. See PalW XXIV, p. 72, system 2, m. 3; p. 73, system 3, m. 5; p. 85, system 3, m. 5; p. 85, system 3, m. 7; p. 86, system 1, m. 2.

This example also shows the use of isolated quarter notes in place of accented half notes,[42] a feature that one meets in early Palestrina compositions fairly frequently; also the use of portamento dissonances of the third, which are, however, frequently derived from the model composition by Josquin; and also the relatively abundant use of sequences—for example:

Ex. 15 [43]

et re - sur - re - xit ter - ti - a di -

In this last connection the Mass *Benedicta* strongly approaches the Mass *Ut re mi fa sol la,* which contains a very striking sequence in the Sanctus (indeed, twice):

Ex. 16

Sa - - - - - - - - etc.

Another and still more definite criterion of stylistic proximity between the two Masses is offered by the themes of the two Masses:

Ex. 17

De - um de De - - - o   in no - - mi - ne

These two themes seem to be the only instances in which Palestrina uses a group of four eighth notes (which are extremely rare in his music in *alla breve* meter) as material for thematic development.

Still closer seems the stylistic connection between the Mass *Benedicta* and the *Pope Marcellus Mass.* Strongly suggestive is the use of the freely syncopated dissonance in quarter-note duration—for instance, —which is not yet visible in the First Book of Masses, but appears in these two Masses more frequently than anywhere else in Palestrina's

---

42. See, for example, apart from the theme given above, PalW **XXIV**, p. 101, system 3, mm. 2, 4. A characteristic case in the Mass *Ad coenam agni providi* of the First Book of Masses may also be cited:

Et in - car - na - - - tus

43. The Christe theme cited above also exhibits sequential motion.

Ex. 18

works; even where it is found elsewhere, it normally appears only once in a given composition. An exception to this is the five-voice motet *Surge Petre* (Pal W IV, p. 130), in which it appears twice through repetition; further and more significant examples are found in the *Pope Marcellus Mass* (four occurrences) and the Mass *Benedicta* (five occurrences). Furthermore, only in these two Masses is it used in a way that sets it off from surrounding material, with intervals of a few measures.

The passage Qui sedes in the *Benedicta* Mass was transposed to Ionian when taken over into the *Pope Marcellus Mass,* but was otherwise little changed. That the derivation does not go in the opposite direction, and that the passage as it appears in the *Pope Marcellus Mass* is the borrowed one, is easy to see; the whole basis for the formula is closely bound up with the principal theme of the Mass *Benedicta:*

Ex. 19 [44]

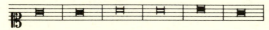

One finds this theme not only as *cantus firmus* in the alto, but the soprano melody is also derived from it. As is customary in Palestrina, the Qui sedes of the Gloria of the *Benedicta* Mass begins a new section in which, as in many other Masses, its material is developed from the opening motive of the Mass. This theme is particularly prominent in the upper voice of the Gloria, as in these examples:

Ex. 20

Et in＿＿ ter - ra pax ho- Do - mi - ni fi - li Qui tol -lis pec - ca - ta＿＿ mun - di＿＿

It is apparent, then, that the passage in the Mass *Benedicta* is the original one. This inference is strengthened by the fact that the Christe of the *Pope Marcellus Mass* is isolated in the Mass in its use of this opening

44. As remarked earlier, this theme is derived from a liturgical melody.

formula. The procedure of using two outer voices in tenths with an immobile middle voice appears in no other Christe setting by Palestrina, and it helps to characterize the Christe of the *Pope Marcellus Mass* as a borrowing. When, in addition, one considers the old-fashioned features of the entire *Benedicta,* it appears to be clear that the *Pope Marcellus Mass* could have been written only after the Mass *Benedicta.*

The question remains: How long after the earlier Mass one may place the *Pope Marcellus Mass?* As mentioned earlier, Cardinal Truchsess wrote on November 8, 1562, to say that the Mass *Benedicta* "was composed in the past few days" (*dise tag gemacht*). The close stylistic connection between this Mass and the *Pope Marcellus Mass,* and the further connection to the Mass *Ut re mi fa sol la* of 1562, makes it more than probable that the *Pope Marcellus Mass* was also written in the second half of 1562 or early in 1563. The stylistic unevenness of these two Masses does not make so narrow a chronological relationship necessarily improbable, for the *Pope Marcellus Mass* may have marked a sudden breakthrough to the mature Palestrina style. On the other hand, we may exclude the possibility that after writing the *Pope Marcellus Mass,* Palestrina could have turned back to so retrospective a work as the Mass *Benedicta.*

In my book *The Style of Palestrina and the Dissonance* (original edition, 1925), I summarized my studies of text intelligibility in Palestrina's Masses as follows:

> Doubtless Palestrina was more concerned about making the words as intelligible as possible in the *Pope Marcellus Mass* than he was in any of his other Masses; the style of the *Pope Marcellus Mass* is not the result of purely musical considerations, but is also determined by outwardly imposed practical requirements. . . . That this style of writing is so fully carried through in the *Pope Marcelleus Mass* must undoubtedly be regarded as having a connection with the musical-liturgical viewpoint enunciated by the Council of Trent (whatever the particular circumstances of composition of the Mass may have been).

It now occurs to me that the *Pope Marcellus Mass* is to be seen as a composition for a particular occasion, and, indeed, that the derivation of the passage from the Mass *Benedicta* is most simply explained psychologically as the consequence of the composer's working in haste and under pressure to finish it. With this view in mind, its probable date of composition would be between the twenty-second and twenty-fourth sessions of the council, when matters of church music were on the agenda at Trent.

It appears to me that the claim made by the Jesuit Cresollio (who in 1629 wrote an account that was, he said, reported by a member of his religious order, who had heard it personally from Palestrina) is supported by the foregoing discussion—namely, Cresollio's claim that Pius IV was ready to request the Council of Trent to abolish church polyphony, and that he had already spoken with several cardinals and other prelates on the matter. Palestrina then convinced the pope, through the composition of several Masses, that it was possible, despite contemporary artistic requirements, to compose in such a way that the text remained intelligible and the music remained pious and worthy.[45] It also seems to me plausible to accept Guidiccioni's communication, that Cardinal Rodolfo Pio, who had been the enemy of church music at the council, was persuaded otherwise by works of Palestrina,[46] especially when one considers that in 1563 Palestrina dedicated his First Book of Motets for Four Voices to this cardinal, perhaps to thank him for his support. In consequence there seems to me to be no doubt that the *Pope Marcellus Mass* can be assigned to the years 1562–63, and that it was indeed written in connection with the Council of Trent.

45. *Ludovici Cresollii Mystagogus,* Paris, 1629. [See Reading 11. *Editor*]
46. Guidiccioni's letter to Bishop Suarez on February 17, 1637; edition published Rome, 1655, p. 285. Baini's claim, that Cardinal Pio was not personally present at the council is pointless, since he could easily have sent the Mass to the council through an emissary, as was done by Cardinal Truchsess von Waldburg with de Kerle's *Preces Speciales*. See Ursprung, *op. cit.,* p. 19. [See Reading 12. *Editor*]

VIEWS
AND COMMENTS

In this section, all footnotes are by the editor.

GIOVANNI BATTISTA MARTINI

~~~

[*From* Saggio fondamentale pratico di contrappunto] †

It is to be observed in Palestrina that since he had studied the works of his predecessors not only of the sixteenth century, in which he lived, but also of the preceding century, he was able to put to use a great variety of artifices introduced by them. To this he added his singular skill in cleansing them and purging them of a certain awkwardness and weakness caused not only by the somewhat unfortunate taste of those times, but also by the heavy density of their style, to which they attached great importance. . . . Palestrina, however, knew how to purge the art of counterpoint of such imperfections and introduce fullness of harmony, proportioned grace, and a truly pleasing melody in every part which would not incommode the singer, thus forming a perfect whole.

†Full title: *Esemplare ossia saggio fondamentale pratico di contrappunto sopra il canto fermo,* Bologna, 1774, pp. 51 f. Translated by the editor.

E. T. A. HOFFMANN

[*From* Alte und neue Kirchenmusik] †

A reconciliation with art was made by Pope Marcellus II, who at first was persuaded to the view that all music should be banned from the church. Thus religion would have been robbed of its highest glory had not the great master, Palestrina, restored to it the holy wonder of musical art in its inmost being. From then on music became the truest means of worship in the Catholic church; and so there arose at the time the deepest understanding of the inner nature of music in the pious soul of the masters, and in true holy exaltation their immortal and inimitable songs streamed forth. The six-voice Mass that Palestrina composed at that time (in 1555)[1] to permit the perplexed pope to hear true music and which bears his name (*Missa Papae Marcelli*) has become very famous.

With Palestrina there arose unquestionably the most splendid period of church music (and of music in general) that for nearly two centuries held sway in ever-increasing richness of piety and strength. Yet it is not to be denied that already in the first century after Palestrina high and inimitable simplicity and dignity was lost in a certain elegance toward which the masters strove.

It is altogether fitting and necessary here to look deeper into the nature of the music of this patriarch of music. Lacking all embellishment and all melodic flights, it presents for the most part a succession of perfect consonant harmonies, the force and boldness of which grip the

† This excerpt is reprinted in Hoffmann's *Schriften zur Musik; Nachlese*, Munich, 1963, pp. 214–17. The article was originally published in the *Allgemeine Musikalische Zeitung*, Jg. XVI (September, 1814), and was included by Hoffmann in the second volume of his *Serapions-Brüder*, published in 1819. The present translation is by the editor.

1. In the 1819 version of this essay Hoffmann questioned whether the date 1555 was correct; his doubt was evidently based on the appearance in 1814 of E. L. Gerber's *Neues Hist.-biog. Lexikon der Tonkünstler*, II, 3. Teil, p. 645, in which the date of publication of the Second Book of Masses is given, correctly, as 1567.

spirit with inexpressible power and raise it to the highest sphere. Love, the union of all that is holy in nature, as it was promised to the Christians, expresses itself in this harmony, which thus awoke for the first time in Christendom; and the chord and the harmony form the image and expression of the spiritual community, the union with the eternal and ideal, that is enthroned above us but yet encompasses us. From the purest, holiest, and most religious feelings must such music come, which arises only as expression of that love, ignoring and scorning all that is worldly. Thus Palestrina's simple and dignified works were conceived in the highest strength of piety and love, and they propagate the divine with power and splendor. To his music is really suited what the Italians say of the works of many composers who in comparison to him are shallow and weak: it is truly music from another world. The flow of the single voices is reminiscent of plainsong; seldom do they exceed the range of a sixth and never does an awkward interval appear or one that, as they say, does not lie well in the throat. It goes without saying that in keeping with the practice of his time Palestrina wrote for voices alone, without the accompaniment of any instruments: for the praise of the highest and holiest should stream forth from the breasts of men without any intervening medium, and without the admixture of any foreign element.

The succession of perfect consonant triads, especially in minor keys, has become so strange to us—in our debilitated state—that many, to whose taste the sacred sphere is entirely closed, see nothing in it but poverty of technical structure. In that regard, even apart from every higher aspect, and considering only what in common circles is customarily called "effect," it is perfectly plain that in the church—in the vast inner spaces of cathedrals—it is precisely the intermingling of elements through passage work and short passing tones that breaks down the effect of music by rendering it unintelligible. In Palestrina's music every chord strikes the listener with the same force, and the most intricate tonal structures will never be able to make so striking an effect as those bold, powerful chords which break in upon the mind like streaming rays.

Palestrina is simple, steadfast, childlike, pious, strong, and mighty— truly Christian in his work, like the painter Pietro di Cortona and our old Dürer. Composing for him was in itself religious practice.

RICHARD WAGNER

[*From the* Entwurf zur Organisation eines deutschen Nationaltheaters 1849] †

If Catholic church music is to be maintained properly under the conditions that currently prevail, at least in the Catholic church at Dresden, it will have to have restored to it the almost completely lost attribute of religious loftiness and fervor. Pope Marcellus in the sixteenth century wanted to ban music completely from the church, for the scholastic and speculative character of church music at the time threatened the devoutness and piety of religious expression. Palestrina saved church music from the ban by restoring to it this essential expressive character. His works and those of his school and of the century after him bear in them the flower and highest perfection of Catholic church music: they are written for performance only by human voices. The first step in the decline of true Catholic church music was the introduction of orchestral instruments into it; through this and through their increasingly freer and more independent use, a sensuous element was thrust upon religious expression, thereby sorely injuring it and exercising a most dangerous influence upon church music. The virtuosity of the instrumentalists required eventually the same virtuosity of the singers, and soon secular operatic tastes fully penetrated into the church. Certain religious texts, such as 'Christe eleison," were stamped as standard texts for operatic arias, and well-trained singers were drawn into the churches to sing them according to the fashionable Italian style of the day. . . .

† This article has been reprinted in Richard Wagner, *Sämtliche Schriften und Dichtungen*, 6th ed., Leipzig, 1912–14, II, p. 254. The translation is by Lewis Lockwood.

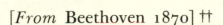

[*From* Beethoven 1870] ††

If we would imagine the truest dream-image of the world in its most faithful representation, we might be able to do so in the most intuitive way if we listen to that famous church composition by Palestrina.[1] Here the rhythm is only perceptible through the changes of harmony in the chordal succession; apart from this, as a symmetrical time succession, it does not exist. The temporal flow here is accordingly so closely bound up with the innately nontemporal and nonspatial nature of the harmony, that the aid of the laws of time is not to be used for the understanding of such music. The time succession in such a work expresses itself only in the slight changes of a basic color, which the manifold ramifications, while maintaining their relationships, display to us, even though we are unable to discern a linear pattern in these changes. But since the color itself does not appear in the spatial dimension, what we receive is an almost timeless and spaceless impression, a spiritual revelation, by which we are gripped with an emotion that is inexpressible because it conveys to our consciousness more clearly than any other experience the inner character of religion freed of all dogmatic fictional content.

†† *Ibid.*, IX, p. 79. Translated by Lewis Lockwood.

1. Wagner is apparently referring to Palestrina's *Stabat mater,* which he had arranged for solo voices and chorus in Dresden in 1848, and which he had performed there for the first time on March 8, 1848. It was first published in 1877; see Liszt's letter to Franz Witt, dated January 20, 1873, in which Liszt mentions that Wagner had given him the manuscript of this arrangement in Zurich "eighteen years ago" (that is, in 1855).

AUGUST WILHELM AMBROS †

~⌇⌇~

[*From* Geschichte der Musik] †

The *Missa Papae Marcelli* opens a new era in the master's work. When one recalls the circumstances that impelled him to compose it, one cannot but admire the skill with which Palestrina reconciled the external requirement—that the text be made clearly perceptible—with the ineluctable requirements of art, indeed of rich artistic forms. Nowhere did he avoid the forbidden "fugues" (i.e., canons): in the Kyrie I itself he set the two basses strictly as a unison canon, while in the Et in terra the two voices are set in an ingenious pseudo-canon; without imitating one another exactly, they answer one another in similar phrases. Where no doubt can exist about a particular word of the text, as at "Amen" and the like, Palestrina grasps the welcomed opportunity to create a more artful interweaving of voices. The entrance of such moments is carefully prepared: the textually dense Credo begins in the simplest manner and becomes gradually more complex until, at the closing "Amen," a richly imitative, lively, and active tonal interplay occurs, the theme of which is created from the descending scale—it is as if rays of harmony descend from heaven. To make the text as clearly understandable as possible, Palestrina often uses note-against-note counterpoint, or he enlivens such combinations by the simplest means: two notes against a short energetic motion of four notes in this or that voice; or while one voice moves in figuration on a syllable of text, he pits a second voice against it with the

---

† Vol. IV (1878), 28. Present translation by the editor. August Wilhelm Ambros (1816–76) was one of the great pioneers of musicology in the nineteenth century, and his *History of Music* (4 vols., 1862–78; fifth volume with musical examples edited by Otto Kade, 1882) stands as the first great effort of the modern era to write a comprehensive and truly scholarly history of music from earliest times to the period of the writer. On Ambros, see Guido Adler, *August Wilhelm Ambros*, in *The Musical Quarterly*, XVII (1931), 360–73, and Phillipp Naegele, *August Wilhelm Ambros: His Historical and Critical Thought*, Diss., Princeton University, 1956.

clearest possible declamation of text and with a characteristic motif. Words like "suscipe," "Miserere," "quoniam," "etiam," "spiritum," "resurrectione," "venturi saeculi," he declaims in the most careful manner and in the clearest way; they stand out as if they were written in etched block letters in a lapidary style. Palestrina organizes the voices frequently in groups of three or four—when all six voices enter it creates a powerful effect of contrast in tonal strength without in any way lessening clarity. All these means are found in works by Palestrina's predecessors; but his achievement seems greater, not less, when one realizes with what imagination he chose from all sides precisely those things that would best serve the purpose established for him.

This work has customarily been regarded as Palestrina's highest achievement, but among the other Palestrina Masses there are many that equal it in value and beauty. Characteristic of this work is an unusual degree of simplicity. In the interweaving of the six voices the writing throughout is masterly, lively, and of ideal purity. It is quite understandable that the *Missa Papae Marcelli* made a sensation among Palestrina's contemporaries. . . .

GIUSEPPE VERDI

~~~~

[Letter to Giuseppe Gallignani 1891] †

I am sorry not to have been able to attend your concerts of sacred music. I know that they were well received and am glad of it. I am particularly pleased about the performance of the music of Palestrina, the true prince of sacred music, and the "eternal father" of Italian music.

With the daring harmonic discoveries of modern music one cannot compose in the manner of Palestrina, it is true; but if he were better known and studied, we would write in a more Italian manner and we would be better patriots (in music, of course). . . .

† From *I Copialettere di Giuseppe Verdi*, ed. by G. Cesari and A. Luzio, Milan, 1913, letter CCCXLIV, dated Milan, November 15, 1891, and translated for this volume by Lewis Lockwood. Its recipient, Giuseppe Gallignani, had previously been director of music at the Duomo of Milan, and had recently been appointed director of the Conservatory of Music at Parma.

Bibliography

GENERAL WORKS ON SIXTEENTH-CENTURY MUSIC

Besseler, H., *Die Musik des Mittelalters und der Renaissance,* Potsdam, 1931.

Blume, F., *Renaissance and Baroque Music,* New York, 1967.

Einstein, A., *The Italian Madrigal,* 3 vols., Princeton, 1949.

Hughes, Dom A., and G. Abraham, *The New Oxford History of Music,* vol. 3: *Ars Nova and the Renaissance, 1300–1540,* London, 1960; vol. 4: *The Age of Humanism, 1504–1630,* London, 1968.

La Rue, J., ed., *Aspects of Medieval and Renaissance Music: A Birthday Offering to Gustave Reese,* New York, 1966.

Pirro, A., *Histoire de la musique de la fin du XIVe siècle à la fin du XVIe,* Paris, 1940.

Reese, G., *Music in the Renaissance,* New York, 1954; rev. ed., 1959.

Strunk, O., *Source readings in Music History,* New York, 1950.

Wolff, H. C., *Die Musik der Alten Niederländer,* Leipzig, 1956.

GENERAL WORKS ON PALESTRINA

Baini, G., *Memorie storico-critiche della vita e delle opere di Giovanni Pierluigi da Palestrina,* 2 vols., Rome, 1828. See pp. 34 f.

Coates, H., *Palestrina,* London, 1938. [A useful short biography in English.]

Fellerer, K. G., *Palestrina: Leben und Werk,* 2nd rev. ed., Düsseldorf, 1960.

Ferraci, E., *Il Palestrina,* Rome, 1960. [A recent summary of the known biographical data.]

Jeppesen, K., *Palestrina,* in *Die Musik in Geschichte und Gegenwart,* Band X (1962), cols. 658–706. [The most exhaustive survey of his career to date, and the first catalogue listing not only Palestrina's works, but their known sources.]

Ursprung, O., *Palestrina und Palestrina-Renaissance,* in *Zeitschrift für Musikwissenschaft,* VII (1925), 513–29. [An important contribution to the historiography of Palestrina.]

141

PALESTRINA'S TECHNIQUE AND STYLE

Andrews, H. K., *An Introduction to the Technique of Palestrina*, London, 1958.
Apfel, E., *Zur Entstehungsgeschichte des Palestrinasatzes*, in *Archiv für Musikwissenschaft*, XIV (1957), 30–45.
Bellermann, H., *Der Kontrapunkt*, Berlin, 1862.
Hermelink, S., *Dispositiones Modorum*, Tutzing, 1960. See p. 80.
Jeppesen, K., *The Style of Palestrina and the Dissonance*, 2nd ed., London, 1946. [An exhaustive study of Palestrina's contrapuntal technique.]
―――― *Counterpoint*, New York, 1939. [A teaching manual based on the preceding volume.]

STUDIES OF THE PALESTRINA MASSES AND OF THE *Pope Marcellus Mass*

Bobbitt, R., *Harmonic Tendencies in the Missa Papae Marcelli*, in *The Music Review*, XVI (1955), 273–88.
Haberl, F. X., *Die Cardinalskommission von 1564 und Palestrinas Missa Papae Marcelli*, in *Kirchenmusikalisches Jahrbuch*, VII (1892), 82–97.
Jeppesen, K., *Wann entstand die Marcellus-Messe*, in *Festschrift für Guido Adler*, Vienna, 1930, pp. 126–36. [Reprinted in the following item.]
―――― *Marcellus-Probleme*, in *Acta Musicologica*, XVI–XVII (1944–45), 11–38. [Complete translation presented in this edition.]
Klassen, J., *Untersuchungen zur Parodiemesse Palestrinas*, in *Kirchenmusikalisches Jahrbuch*, XXXVII (1953), 53–63.
―――― *Das Parodieverfahren in der Messe Palestrinas*, in *Kirchenmusikalisches Jahrbuch*, XXXVIII (1954), 24–54.
―――― *Zur Modellbehandlung in Palestrinas Parodiemessen*, in *Kirchenmusikalisches Jahrbuch*, XXXIX (1955), 41–55.
Marshall, R. L., *The Paraphrase Technique of Palestrina in His Masses Based on Hymns*, in *Journal of the American Musicological Society*, XVI (1963), 347–72.
Schnürl, K., *Die Variationstechnik in den Choral-Cantus firmus-Werken Palestrinas*, in *Studien zur Musikwissenschaft*, XXIII (1956), 11–66.
Wagner, P., *Geschichte der Messe*, Leipzig, 1913.
Weinmann, K., *Zur Geschichte der Palestrinas Missa Papae Marcelli*, in *Jahrbuch der Musikbibliothek Peters*, XXIII (1916), 23–42.